"Brandolon's journey and his quest for an important read for all of us mother, I am touched deeply by Brandolon's anguish over his mom's death and his establishment of the Gwendolyn Smith Charitable Fund as his own foundation and expression of his unconditional love. Brandolon will continue to be a powerful force for good and make his own global impact."

—Scott Jackson
president and CEO, Global Impact

"*Dreams Deferred* is an important read about the experiences of a Black man working in the social sector. Brandolon's poignant and often humorous stories illustrate the tensions held by many people of color in that sector and serve as a reminder that real social progress requires unique perspectives that can only be achieved through diverse leadership."

—Edgar Villanueva
author, activist, and philanthropist

"Brandolon's story is a must-read that provides perspective, not only on struggle during a recession, but on thriving under challenging circumstances and maintaining a passion for one's dreams—in his case, dreams of social impact and creating a more equitable world. I, for one, can't wait to see how his story continues, because I know this is just the beginning."

—Carolyn Nissen
*Deputy Director of Development, Advancement Project
National Office*

"In this time of racial reckoning in the United States, *Dreams Deferred* is a timely, as well as poignant, personal story. A must-read for anyone who wants to learn more about how new ways of giving are changing our understanding of philanthropy and to believe that, despite personal and financial struggles, anyone can find success and hope through work that doesn't merely pay the bills, but actively makes the world a better place."

—Dr. Una Osili
PhD, Associate Dean for Research and International Programs, IU Lilly Family School of Philanthropy

RECESSION, STRUGGLE, AND THE
QUEST FOR A BETTER WORLD

Dreams Deferred

BRANDOLON BARNETT

Advantage.

Published by Advantage, Charleston, South Carolina.
Member of Advantage Media Group.

ADVANTAGE is a registered trademark, and the Advantage colophon is a trademark of Advantage Media Group, Inc.

Printed in the United States of America.

10 9 8 7 6 5 4 3 2 1

ISBN: 978-1-64225-216-3
LCCN: 2021902716

Cover design by David Taylor.
Layout design by Mary Hamilton.

This publication is designed to provide accurate and authoritative information in regard to the subject matter covered. It is sold with the understanding that the publisher is not engaged in rendering legal, accounting, or other professional services. If legal advice or other expert assistance is required, the services of a competent professional person should be sought.

Advantage Media Group is proud to be a part of the Tree Neutral® program. Tree Neutral offsets the number of trees consumed in the production and printing of this book by taking proactive steps such as planting trees in direct proportion to the number of trees used to print books. To learn more about Tree Neutral, please visit www.treeneutral.com.

Advantage Media Group is a publisher of business, self-improvement, and professional development books and online learning. We help entrepreneurs, business leaders, and professionals share their Stories, Passion, and Knowledge to help others Learn & Grow. Do you have a manuscript or book idea that you would like us to consider for publishing? Please visit advantagefamily.com or call 1.866.775.1696.

I dedicate this book to my mother, Gwendolyn Louise Smith. I owe you more than I could ever communicate. All I can say is, Thank you.

Also, to those who've supported me through dark times and happy celebrations: Dr. James Evans, student dean at the University of Pittsburgh at Bradford; my truest brother, William Kim; and Messay Derebe, my greatest friend, partner, and love.

Finally, I also dedicate this to the District Karaoke crew, home to an entire community of friends who have supported me, and anyone who loves and makes beautiful music. I'd be lost without it.

CONTENTS

FOREWORD

K. James Evans

I first came to know the author of this remarkable book when he enrolled in 2003 as a freshman at the University of Pittsburgh at Bradford, where I served as dean of students. From Brandolon Barnett's earliest days in college, I would see a young man seated alone at breakfast in the corner of the college dining room, and I would frequently join him. A friendship developed between us. I told him about the Semester at Sea program I would be leading as executive dean in the fall of 2004 and that if he took part, he could travel on a hundred-day academic voyage around the world as a member of a floating college campus community, taking classes while at sea and visiting ports in Asia, the Indian subcontinent, Africa, and South America. I further explained how, even with his limited financial resources, scholarship help was available. He applied, was awarded scholarships, and embarked on his voyage in August of that year.

My friendship with Brandolon was made possible by my own experience as a first-generation college student. I was fortunate to have been born into a family in which higher education was deemed important. When I went off to college in the 1960s, there were a number of role models there who had a tremendous influence on my developing a sense of vocation. Chief among them was the college's dean of students, whom I knew to be an individual who quietly and without fanfare helped many students sort through personal issues, remain in college, graduate, and go on to live productive, contributive, and meaningful lives. By my senior year in college, I committed myself to pursue the same line of work. Not too many years later, I realized my dream and for forty-two years held the position of dean of students at the University of Pittsburgh at Bradford.

As the dean, I tried to assist as many students as I could along their individual paths, much as my own dean from years before had done for me and others. Looking back now from the perspective of one who is "retired," I see that I could not have chosen any other life's work—perhaps, just possibly, it chose me. Working with students like Brandolon has been for me one of life's greatest joys. If I made any impact on Brandolon Barnett, it was truly my humble honor and a result of my calling to the student affairs vocation, as well as the close personal friendship we developed with one another.

Semester at Sea gave Brandolon the confidence and courage to travel on his own to other parts of the world after graduation and to ultimately move to London, where he studied and earned the master's degree. That said, the path forward for him would still be far from easy. As Brandolon looked for internships and jobs that would provide him not only with meaning but also with an income he could live on, he would find his path to be full of obstacles, made even worse by the recession of 2008.

Through all these challenges, Brandolon Barnett succeeded, and I believe the story of his young adult years can serve as a beacon of hope to those who find similar challenges during that same period of their lives. The themes of *Dreams Deferred* are many—resilience, flexibility, frustration, motivation, the importance of friendships, despair, love, and hope. But perhaps the most important underlying theme is the consistency of a mother's love for her son and how she sacrificed in so many ways to make sure he could make it in the world.

My own life has been deeply enriched by coming to know Brandolon. He is a man of substance and integrity, as evidenced by his continued work in organizations that seek to build a better world, which was the goal he set for himself while in college years ago. He has written a book of honest storytelling about every step of his journey. To my knowledge, there is no book quite like this one—detailing as it does a young Black man's struggle to survive the Great Recession and come out the other side with his dreams intact. By reading his book, you will find inspiration and hope from the struggles and victories of a young man who, through it all, still has as his guiding light a mission of service to others. If you yourself are struggling and are finding it difficult to make your own way in the world, his story may be just what you need to become more persistent and confident and to not give up as you aspire toward your goal.

—K. James Evans
Bradford, Pennsylvania
November 1, 2020

FOREWORD

Greg Baldwin

There is nothing easier to do in the world than learn how to quit. It is the seductive and often irresistible solution to the disappointments, injustices, and tragedies each of us, in our own way, will inevitably confront.

Dreams Deferred is the remarkable story of a man who had every reason to quit—but did not. It is about a mother's love and a son's journey to prevent poverty, racism, injustice, and doubt from convincing him to give up on himself and on his dreams.

I didn't know any of that when I first met Brandolon Barnett. All I knew was that he was different from other people I met regularly, and as the product manager at Salesforce.org, working on corporate volunteering, one of the many people in Big Tech with the power to crush *my* dreams.

See, I am the CEO of VolunteerMatch, the Oakland-based nonprofit behind the web's largest volunteer engagement network.

I've had hundreds of meetings in Silicon Valley with Big Tech product managers over the past decade, but most of them don't go anywhere. Sometimes, it's because there are easier ways to make money online than partnering with a nonprofit to more effectively connect volunteers with the nonprofits who need them. But most of the time, it is because companies with thousands of engineers can't possibly imagine how they might need VolunteerMatch to help them solve anything.

Brandolon, as you'll learn, has a very different perspective than what I'd grown accustomed to. He seemed to understand more about nonprofits and asked better questions. He wanted to know more about the challenges that get in the way of connecting volunteers to the organizations that need them. And he wanted to know *why* I thought VolunteerMatch had succeeded where others had failed. In other words, Brandolon was better informed and more thoughtful than your average "tech bro," but it finally occurred to me that what made Brandolon *really* different was that he actually cared about the problem.

If you don't live in Silicon Valley, that might seem like an odd thing for me to say, because one of Big Tech's greatest strengths has been its extraordinary capacity to scale new solutions to old problems. Tragically, its greatest weakness has been a single-minded indifference to caring about problems its employees didn't have. As a result, most of the digital technology we enjoy today was designed, funded, and built by people to solve the problems that they knew, not the ones they didn't. What makes Brandolon so special is that he knows and cares about problems they don't have in Silicon Valley—and hasn't given up on his dream to fix them.

So, it is my honor to introduce you to the story of Brandolon Barnett, because I hope it will help you hang on to your dreams. I hope it will help you find the courage to learn from your mistakes without giving up, the tenacity to confront discrimination without giving up, and the humility to endure setbacks and tragedies without giving up.

Mostly I hope Brandolon's story will bring together people who care to hang on to the dream that we can, and must, find better ways to serve each other and solve the problems that matter most.

—Greg Baldwin
CEO, VolunteerMatch

CHAPTER ONE

ROCK BOTTOM

There I was, in a position I never imagined I'd be in. It was September of 2013. My every step was haunted by trepidation. My insides twisted nervously. I was scared, but some part of my mind was still stubbornly defiant.

My story is not an uncommon one. In fact, from 2008 to 2013, lots of people found themselves in positions they never expected: lining up to get payday loans, signing up for Medicaid, needing food stamps.

Me? I was walking through downtown San Francisco.

San Francisco was as beautiful as ever, as wistful as any vacation memory or picture postcard. I walked, keenly aware of the life that filled the city, noticing that the place (at least the part I was walking through) was "Blacker" than I had expected. As a Black southerner from Dallas, I found the city somewhat surreal. The people I overheard here spoke differently than Blacks in the South but with the same general tenor and sans that sometimes dubious southern friendliness—a friendliness I nevertheless occasionally missed. As I walked along, I took in the whole community. Folks of all stripes gathered at trolley stops, basking in the late summer sun. Conversations, liveliness … and there—as I headed down Market Street toward the Tenderloin—San Francisco City Hall came into view. A grand dome, ornate even from a distance.

It was a world all its own, a sublime urbanity that I had craved like so many others of my generation, tired of the tyranny of the automobile and exhausted by the suburban mindset and being isolated from other human beings. Here was life, beauty, possibility, messiness, energy, and fun—here was a place in which I might someday belong. Indeed, San Francisco appeared to me as a gorgeous construct of wide avenues and interesting alleyways.

One of those alleyways might even serve as my bed that evening.

Here was Life, Beauty, Possibility, messiness, energy, and Fun—Here was a Place in WHicH I migHT someday Belong.

I'd made a gamble that day before boarding the Caltrain in the early morning at the Sunnyvale station on the outskirts of San Jose. My two-day-a-week ride to and from the city for my unpaid internship cost fourteen dollars. I'd stood at the fare machine in the chill morning hours, trying again and again to pay, my debit card repeatedly rejected. Nine of the fourteen dollars meant to get me to and from work that day had gone to a Netflix account I was certain I'd canceled. I backed up from the machine to let others have their go, watched as they paid and moved on with their mornings. These were people with money. People with paid jobs and not dwindling savings and a small pension. In that moment, I marveled at their ability to do something so effortlessly that was for me not at all simple. Such is life—alternatingly banal and frightening.

I got on the phone to Chase Bank.

"May I ask who I am speaking with?" She sounded really cute. At least I imagined she was cute; nay, hot. And in a few moments, she would see … just how devastatingly broke and pathetic I was.

"Brandolon Barnett," I choked out.

"Thank you, sir. And for security purposes, can you verify the last four digits of your social security number and date of birth."

I listed off the numbers and added: "I'm a Scorpio." I choked out that last sad and awkward attempt at humor. She didn't laugh. It wasn't funny.

"Thank you, sir. And just so that you know, this call may be recorded for training and quality assurance purposes. How may I help you today?"

"Well, I'm pretty sure I canceled my Netflix account, but it seems they charged me in error this morning, and I was hoping that I could get you to reject the charge."

"Certainly, sir. I can take care of that for you."

"That easy? Thanks."

"Certainly. I've gone ahead and rejected the pending charge, and your balance should reflect this change within twenty-four hours."

"Thank you."

That's all I said to the cute-sounding bank representative. Thank you. What I really needed to know was that the money would be there when it was time to head home at five o'clock. Yet having already had some experience with desperation and banks (too often intertwined),

I knew she wouldn't be able to tell me for sure. And even if she did have an answer, she could be wrong. It's not as if there would be consequences for JPMorgan Chase if some down-on-his-luck Black millennial hipster dude had stupidly relocated to a metropolitan area so expensive it might as well be Monaco and got stuck sleeping on the streets of San Francisco in his slim (not skinny) jeans and sneakers. But hey, at least I had an unpaid internship to which I could wear my slim jeans and sneakers from H&M.

I try to look on the bright side. Occasionally.

I was at a fork in the road, and I had a choice to make. The story of my life.

I could use my last $7.20 for a one-way ticket and hope the money appeared by day's end. Or I could miss one of the sixteen days at my internship, my two-month chance at a career correction and a better life. Timidly sliding up to the ticketing machine, I made a gamble.

Ten hours later I was shuffling the streets of San Francisco's Tenderloin neighborhood, in that position I never imagined I could be in, thinking to myself: The degrees? They won't cushion my ass from the concrete. The hardships I've overcome? They don't make a great meal. And so, amid all the beauty and energy of that place, I walked with twisted insides, knowing my fate, for this day, lay in the hands of big American finance. The irony.

CHAPTER TWO

LUCKY SEVENS

From the time I was a small child, I lived my life so that it would make a good *story*. I don't remember when exactly it began. Perhaps it was the books we read as children in English classes, or the infinitely superior sci-fi of Clarke and Asimov that consumed me in my free time. Regardless how it happened, at some point in my formative years, I came to hold an almost religious view about the fundamental importance of a good story.

In that view, one thing was beyond certain. No one revels in the tale about the person born with a silver spoon in his or her mouth, who is as brilliant as everyone always knew they would be, is talented at everything, marries, has the perfect number of children (2.3), and wins the geek triple crown: a Nobel, a MacArthur genius award, and a Pulitzer. Of course, they do all that during a thirty-year stint in the US Senate, after which they finish their career as a caring ambassador and/or philanthropist who ultimately dies peacefully asleep at home. *That* story is boring and exhausting. I truly believe it's the details, the struggle, our quirks and superstitions, and the adversity that we overcome that make our stories worth telling. They're particularly worth telling when doing so just might help someone else avoid making the same mistakes or inspire another to persevere through their own trials and tribulations, knowing that others have made it through to the other side.

That's why I tell my story. And why I hope it's a good one.

My first day of work after college came in June 2007. I was twenty-two years old. It was a hot and sunny summer day in Dallas. Cottonwood fragments floated in the air. As was usual for the area, there was not a single cloud in the sky. It was one of those days when you'd be forgiven for thinking shade could be treated as a currency. Most importantly, to me at least, *it was 2007.*

You see, seven is my lucky number. I'm actually completely convinced that important things happen to me on days with a seven. And minutes with a seven. And when there are seven people in the room. When I spend seven dollars. When something takes seven seconds. The beauty of superstition is the surety and faith it can inspire for what's utterly unreasonable. How fitting then, for my life and career as an adult to begin in earnest in 2007. I'm starting off on the right foot! I'll have a great story! I felt kissed by fate, assured that one day Morgan Freeman or a similarly majestic-sounding famous actor would narrate the beginning of my incredible rise: "The year was 2007 …"

I was one of the few among my classmates with a job offer waiting after graduation. With a BA in communications (I was smitten with communications theory!), I knew even then that I was lucky. I'd traveled a long way from Dallas, Texas, up to Bradford and Pittsburgh, Pennsylvania, to get a degree from the University of Pittsburgh. I was proud of that stiff piece of paper marking my achievement.

The nonprofit I would start working for that day was situated in a small office behind the large home of the organization's owner. The home, located in the Dallas neighborhood of Lakewood, was, to my eyes, huge. It was two stories tall on a nice plot of land, and it was well made if not traditionally styled. It represented incredible wealth compared to the world I'd seen growing up in that same city.

At the gate, I entered the code as instructed, sending a huge black fence swinging open onto a gray-graveled driveway with a perfectly manicured green lawn. This was years before I learned the awesome little statistic that Dallas is about the same latitude as Baghdad. Now, of course, with droughts and climate change, polar vortices, and flooding Pacific islands, I see these things through a different lens. But as a creature of apartment buildings and concrete plains and canyons, that lush green lawn was beautiful to me then.

I walked with excitement and nervousness toward the front door. I was as hot as one could be in late May in Texas with added humidity steaming from a lake a five-minute walk away. The soothing sound of crunching gravel faded as I walked up the steps. My knock on the front door was answered by a maid. Or perhaps a nanny. Or both. To be honest, at that time I knew the words but not really the functional distinctions between them.

I was familiar with the inside of the house, thanks to an Exxon-Mobil-sponsored internship I'd completed with the organization the summer before I graduated. Like a giant two-story city-dweller's *cabin*, it was beautifully minimalist, all wood, in a dozen different shades. With its high ceilings and open floor plan, anyone who stepped inside would know that it was a young dwelling, possibly built by the current owners to suit their tastes. To my eyes it represented ultra-wealth, at least in Dallas, Texas. I'd already learned that land and labor are cheaper there than most places and that wealth and status mean different things in different places.

My boss was seated at the kitchen island and greeted me as she looked up from her computer. She flashed a big smile and came over to shake my hand. I smiled back. Due to my habit of overworrying and overthinking, I had not yet developed the ability to smile on demand. I'd been prepping that smile while waiting for the train and on the bus ride over. Thinking back, I was such a serious presence. It wasn't until years later that I would learn the value, and the joy, of small talk, of first meetings, and of forming genuine networks.

Stiffly, I accepted her invitation to come and sit. After I offered my stilted version of pleasantries, she walked me through her expectations. I had two primary responsibilities. First, to produce a short promotional video and use it and other content to promote the company on its new YouTube channel. Some of this filming was to be done on location at the sites of the organization's international volunteer programs. Besides having a background in communications, I also had some international experience from a scholarship-funded trip around the world I'd taken with a program called Semester at Sea. These had qualified me for the gig, in her eyes.

My second responsibility was the real and primary reason I was here. It was what excited me. The organization sent thousands of people and hundreds of thousands of dollars as volunteers or donations to community partners in developing countries. It had programs in Romania, Thailand, Laos, Cambodia, Jamaica, Costa Rica, Brazil, China, and Peru. Yet the organization had no program or presence on the African continent. I was there to change that. I was only twenty-two years old and, at $10.50 an hour, incredibly cheap labor for the work I was being asked to do. A total bargain. The thought that I might not be capable of the job occurred to me about as often as the thought that someone who is capable of it should probably get paid a little more than $10.50 an hour. That is to say: never! I had no context for salary. $50K per year stood out to me as a dream, a milestone that exceeded what almost anyone in my immediate family could imagine earning. Six figures? I would have laughed out of the room anyone who even mentioned such a thing. I could not have imagined ever earning that amount of money, and I certainly had no sense of what various jobs were worth or what a

In my world, you were lucky to have a job, let alone one that didn't make you miserable every day.

person could be paid to do them. In my world, you were lucky to have a job, let alone one that didn't make you miserable every day. No one even talked about having a job that allowed for creativity, problem solving, or building something meaningful.

All I could see at that time was the opportunity to do something valuable.

CHAPTER THREE

THe work
I wanTeD

thers I graduated with went into finance, auditing, STEM fields, or even abroad to teach English. The thought that I was making what some would call "a sacrifice" to work in the NGO (nongovernmental organization) space/nonprofit sector never really entered my mind. I was all about impact, so much so that my interest in making an impact might rightly be labeled a compulsion. That's because I had drawn a connection among several disparate early-life insights. The first had to do with my own struggles. As a child, my eyes had glazed over when my single mother would talk of a world that she felt held her down. A world that made hard work secondary to who you know. A world that imposed limits on her just for being a Black woman. But as I grew up, I learned firsthand the struggles inherent to the simple act of affording an education. I discovered the hardships that could be encountered for even daring to conceive of a dream beyond what one sees and experiences every day.

The second insight was about the sheer magnitude of the burdens borne by others in far-flung communities around the world, burdens that I had barely even read about in books. While I saw my fair share of poverty growing up in South Dallas (a place not exactly known for its wealth and privilege), nothing prepared me for what I saw in college when I participated in the Semester at Sea program. The undoubtedly brilliant child in Vietnam who spoke four languages immaculately but worked the streets guiding tourists and living off their charity. The women stuck for their lifetimes in one of Mother Teresa's Women of Charity convents in India. On that trip around the world as a poor student, I understood for the first time the true depth of human need.

My final epiphany came from watching *Star Trek* and *Babylon 5* and from reading the works of Isaac Asimov and Arthur C. Clarke. My whole life I had loved nothing more than to lose myself in science-fiction stories of far-flung futures. Stories of a humanity capable of claiming even the stars as home. As I grew into adulthood, I couldn't reconcile the suffering I had seen others enduring and the struggles I myself had experienced with what I had dreamed was possible from reading these works. Put simply, how would we ever build a Federation of Planets when we couldn't find ways, with all our ingenuity, to even provide opportunity for those with the talent to contribute across a multitude of fields? How could we truly lay the foundations for broader exploration of the many unknowns in our universe if we were squandering so much human potential? How much genius was priced out, socialized out, smashed out, starved out, or otherwise kept from *awakening* to help us move beyond where we were as a people—as a species?

Making my life a good story came to mean becoming part of the story of shaping a world where things were measurably better. I committed myself to this philosophy. So my hourly rate meant nothing. It was simply the dues I was happy to pay to be engaged in something I could love and that could change the world.

MaKing my Life a good story came to mean Becoming Part of The story of shaping a world where things were measurably Better.

It must also be said: living in a cheap city and at home with my mother and her boyfriend certainly made these lofty ideals easier to keep in view. That was my privilege. To be born in a place with *some* opportunity, some connection to a broader world. Others aren't so lucky. Maybe, too, I was just a typical millennial, dreaming up my own unique justification for following the advice my generation heard *ad nauseum* to find the "job of your dreams." But commit to those lofty aims I did.

During those early days of my working life in Dallas, I would wake, say my greetings to my mom in the early morning (I wanted to be the first person in the office!), and take my two-mile walk to the train station. Then came a quick ten-minute jaunt on the light rail toward downtown. Most people in Dallas, probably in most of the South, hate mass transit. It's slow. It's inefficient. It's dirty. Most insidiously, "it's for poor people." Most people still hate it even today, even though today we are more aware of the reality of climate change and the need for more efficient and varied transit systems. I couldn't have given less of a shit what people thought. I have always loved a good train or bus trip, a nice walk down even empty city streets. My commutes were so much more than the sum of their three or four stops. I liked the buzz of busy people, the strange conversations that I might overhear, and that certain life that energizes the train car even at 7:00 a.m. when it's filled to the brim with droopy, tired stares. I liked approaching downtown Dallas and its majestic modern skyline, looming larger with each stop. Those train rides were part of my daily love affair with urbanity.

I was probably the one person in the city who wanted nothing to do with any car and had no desire to drive. Often, I felt like I was the only twenty-two-year-old within a thousand miles who didn't even have a license and, to be frank, had never seriously considered obtaining one. Of course, I lied about that last part to friends and ladies. As far as they knew, I'd gotten a license at sixteen, and it "expired" mysteriously (full disclosure: I did not take the driving test and obtain a proper driver's license until I was twenty-seven years old, and I did so at the behest of a very lovely woman). I loved that I became friends with Louis, the shuttle driver at my destination station. Funded by the city, the shuttle was a service mainly designed for older people that picked you up at the station or accepted calls for a pickup within its service area for a dollar or so. I reveled in living like I was in a big city, going against the grain of all the drivers on the roads.

Then there was my work at the nonprofit. The video project seemed easy enough. The only tough thing was that the international travel would provide limited opportunities to get good footage. It's not like I would be able to easily go back to the country if I missed important shots. That meant I had to have a pretty good two-column script of how I envisioned the piece coming together in postproduction. With that, I'd ensure that I could get the shots I'd need to tell the story I envisioned—a story of hard volunteer work, preferably manual volunteer labor, mixed with adventure and new connections and reflected in smiling faces and breathtaking views of monuments or natural splendor.

We learn so little in school. Whether it's high school, college, or even graduate school, we're largely cast out into new and deep waters with very little idea of whether or not we are prepared to swim. From my small desk in our small office, I looked out wistfully at that immaculate green lawn, thought about the immensity of what lived outside those walls, and wondered about my own abilities. From student loans to food, I had a lot of basic needs and endured a lot of struggle just making it from one paycheck to the next. Yet I was a little ball of passion, balancing those basic needs with the drive to find the work I wanted. I suppose that's my default state—poised between survival and the desire for more. Yet sitting there, I made sense of that state by believing in the value of maximizing the overlap of my passion with the everyday work I was doing to put food on the table (and pay $1K plus in student loans). As I think back on it now, that attitude has been key to any successes I've had in pursuing my dreams and understanding my true worth.

As I fell deeper into the work and into my adulthood—planning my travels abroad, understanding my script, struggling to support my mother and pay bills all while making that daily commute in the intense heat of another awful Texas summer—I slowly began to think of it all like this:

Let's say I have a maximum of fifty productive hours in any given week. I know some of you reading may think you're supermen or superwomen who can work a hundred hours per week. But science says otherwise, and I would encourage you to treat yourselves kindly. There's a study from Stanford University which states flatly that "productivity per hour declines sharply when a person works more than fifty hours a week" and that "after fifty-five hours, productivity drops so much that putting in any more hours would be pointless."[1] So, like I said, say I have about fifty productive hours per week ...

Of those fifty hours, a full forty of those were taken up by my job. That gave me nine to ten hours a week to do anything productive that connected to my dreams and passions outside of the office.

Running these numbers, I began to see some justification for that pervasive message of the era to "follow your passions." It's not the most helpful phrase, laden as it is with a host of external expectations, judgments, and emotions that can be pretty fraught. Yet as I thought it through, I began to realize that it could actually be interpreted as a crude and simplistic way of describing *efficient work*. Think about it. If I could find ways—any way at all—to *connect* my passions with the work I was doing to cover my student loans and other basic needs, then I would be dramatically *increasing my efficiency* by increasing my *focus on my passions and interests*. I had a choice: I could spend only 20 percent of my productive hours in a week (that nine to ten hours) focused on my passions and the things I needed to do to get the work I wanted and the life I wanted, or I could increase that percentage. For me this meant two things. Every hour I spent understanding economic and political conditions in the countries I would be visiting was relevant for my current work. Also, it was 2 percent more time in which to focus on building skills and knowledge that helped me advance toward the career of foreign travels and adventures, which

---

1   John Pencavel, "The Productivity of Working Hours" (discussion paper, Department of Economics, Stanford Institute for Economic Policy Research, Stanford University, 2013), https://siepr.stanford.edu/sites/default/files/publications/FatiguepaperSIEPRcover_0.pdf.

was my real dream for how I would come to have an impact on the world. My dream was to lead a life as an NGO worker, UN staffer, or State Department foreign service officer. And given my calculations, achieving that dream seemed rather simple and straightforward.

CHAPTER FOUR

one Humanity

The first time I left the country was in 2004; that was also the first time I saw the ocean. I'd traveled to Vancouver from Dallas by way of what I believe to this day is the worst major airport in America: LAX. I was already nervous setting off as a college sophomore on a trip around the world after a summer at home, and that cramped and disorganized mess of semimodern infrastructure only bred more butterflies deep in the pit of my stomach.

What am I doing? As far as I knew, no one in my family had ever left the country. Hell, to my mind, most had never left Texas. But then again, I never knew my father's side of the family. Maybe they were regular Marco Polos. Maybe they felt that yearning that always consumes me—a hunger to constantly see, read, imagine, and experience things unseen and unexperienced. That pang of jealousy that hits every time I watch birds take flight toward far horizons. The intense and almost unbearable envy I *always* feel when driving past an airport and being subjected to the sight of planes taking off into the distance, racing the setting sun, leaving me behind and embarking on glorious adventures. In my mind, the grass is always greener ... I would probably be the first volunteer on a one-way flight to colonize Mars and beyond.

Throughout my life, I have had to nurture that yearning. That unknown majesty, that great big universe just ripe for exploration remains the most consistent medicine for my doldrums. Those future possibilities and journeys, through space, through time, or through the mists of my own imagination, are what save me. Of course, I wasn't fully aware of that then, as a college sophomore heading out on my first big adventure.

So there I was. Hello, ocean. Hello, world. Touching down in exotic Vancouver to begin a trip to twelve countries around the world on a cruise ship billed as a "sailing university."

I'll never forget my first glimpse of the peaks of British Columbia. True mountains. As a child of the Texas plains, in my first lonely year away at college I'd taken the hills of Pennsylvania to be mountains. There in BC, in that moment, I felt a fool staring at these majestic rocks rising into the clouds. The word *awe* is woefully inadequate to describe how it feels to know that you've never seen the top of the world before—that you only imagined you had. I'm still profoundly inspired by my memories of that trip, not just of Vancouver but of all the places we visited, from Canada to Japan to China, Vietnam, Tanzania, South Africa, and Brazil. The images, the colors, the sights, the smells.

Standing at the Golden Pavilion in Kyoto, in awe of the surrounding calm, the reverence, and the deep well of cultural history, I understood heritage in ways that made me yearn to learn more about my own history and culture. Talking with an artist along the side of the road in Dar es Salaam, Tanzania, I learned that art can save lives by offering meaning, supplying a medium for important messages, and providing work. Sitting in Kowloon Park in Hong Kong, racism took on a new meaning for me when my own heart threatened to jump out of my chest as two Black men approached me. I realized I had internalized the very stereotypes that had often been leveled at me. Two friendly guys looking for conversation had induced a panic in me because of nothing more than the color of their skin and how it stood out among the assembled crowd. These and other realizations overwhelmed me in my adventures. They triggered in me the thought of an *us* that exists across the world as one humanity.

That thought fueled me in my work with the NGO. $10.50 an hour be damned. I was making a difference. I was coming to great and profound realizations about my existence and the very nature of work! I was connecting with my larger goals and dreams. Through this job, I would once again be able to travel to new places, see new sights, make new memories.

> THESE reaLizaTions TriggereD in me THE THOUGHT OF an US THAT EXISTS across THE WOrLD as one HumaniTy.

"You have to know it's easy for you. You can get scholarships any time you like," said one of my coworkers in our little three-person domestic office in Dallas. Shannon was bright and generally relaxed, a former Peace Corps volunteer with aspirations similar to those I had latched onto after my Semester at Sea experience. She, too, was interested in becoming a foreign service officer or working in NGOs improving the world or becoming a foreign policy expert strutting proudly through the halls of power at the State Department or the UN, interpreters in tow. She and I had great conversations around topics in international development, economic impact, and the like. This particular afternoon, however, the topic had turned to race.

"There are definitely lots of scholarships for Black students, but I don't know if you can say that makes things easy," I countered from my desk. The conversations with my two coworkers were generally fun! This was 2007. Before Ferguson. Before #BlackLivesMatter. Obama was on the rise, and Trump was a glimmer in America's eyes, the mere host of a mildly entertaining reality TV show that most people, including myself, have still never seen. In 2007, it was just a little bit easier for my colleagues to imagine that African Americans and other minorities had it "easier" than them.

"I don't know about scholarships, but I wish that it had been easier for me to get aid when applying to SMU. They said my family made too much, but it was so expensive," Caroline, my other coworker, chimed in. To this day, Caroline is someone I consider a friend; she's blond and petite with a kind smile and a penchant for operational problem solving. At the nonprofit, she kept the ship running, whereas I was the new guy. The young guy. And this was a memorably awkward conversation that would stay with me for many years.

"Oh, I totally agree. But what's that have to do with race?" I replied. "That's an issue of college costs and student aid requirements."

"Well," Shannon replied, "it's just strange to complain about opportunity. We all have so much opportunity here in the United States. Especially compared to developing countries."

Oh, those moments. Those moments when I didn't know what to say. You know, the ones during which you know you'll figure out the perfect thing to say about ten minutes after whatever annoying exchange is done. And you'll slap your head wishing you could only … think … faster.

I tried my best in the moment: "It's easy to say that, but it's also the case that unemployment is significantly higher for African Americans, even those with the same qualifications as their white counterparts. Scholarships are available, but they don't offset all the other disadvantages." I distinctly recall being uncomfortable, filled with that surprise one feels when one's liberal American friends say things that make you realize they just don't get your perspective. I wanted to say I knew people who'd been arrested and jailed for smoking weed, something Shannon or some of her friends probably did once, twice, or regularly without much, if any, consequence or concern. But yeah, there are some scholarships for the few who survived broken communities and biased justice systems to make it to college. There's some federal aid money or a loan for those who might manage to finish high school—an achievement that I think qualifies as a scientific miracle after a life of toxic stress's documented and devastating effects on the body and mind. Yeah, that totally balances things out.

Of course, I didn't say these things. I couldn't think fast enough. One never can. Shannon went on a bit longer, all very well-meaning. She was right in one thing. There were worse places. And America had opportunities.

I fell deep into pursuing my own, focusing my effort on the Africa program in particular.

There was no set methodology for "creating" one of the company's global volunteer programs. The goal was to work with local partners, NGOs founded in-country to serve the needs of their local community. Beyond that, there was no other documentation. I sat day after day in front of a screen, staring out at the green of that well-manicured lawn. I would need to create a methodology from scratch.

I began by listing criteria in two tiers: necessary features of a partnership with an African NGO, and desirable features. The company made its impact through promotion of mostly unskilled volunteer work conducted over short periods of one to two weeks. At first, I questioned this very model. But I was also driven by my emergent philosophy to bring my passions into every possible aspect of my work. And as I immersed myself into the growing discourse around the practice, I began to see things differently.

The volunteer programs served as advocacy tools, as volunteers became advocates for the foreign aid process. Like the unskilled volunteers at local hospitals, they could serve the cause despite not being doctors or nurses, or in this case skilled NGO staff or development experts. Just as those hospital volunteers would be among the first to donate if a hospital needed financial assistance, these volunteers would be the frontlines for advocacy if local, state, or federal officials in their districts were promoting legislation that might threaten foreign aid.

As I researched and worked, that information made clear one necessary feature of any program I would create. To act as genuine and effective advocates, our volunteers needed to truly experience the development needs within the communities they visited. But simultaneously, the experience needed to be translatable. It couldn't be so different from their norm as to push them away from feeling that they are stakeholders in the process of international economic development, even if they might not be helping the World Bank, USAID, the State Department, or one of the big international NGOs (the worth of which I now regularly question, but we'll get to that in a bit). The places likely to have this feature had to have some modicum of infrastructure; they couldn't be war zones or isolated towns far from transportation networks.

Of course, Africa is not a country. It is a vast and beautiful continent of many cultures and political and economic realities. Knowing that helped me to whittle down my choices for the location of potential volunteer programs as the summer flew by. All the while I scripted and prepared cameras and equipment for the promotional video I'd soon be filming on location to promote the too-infrequently visited Southeast Asia programs.

The days grew unbearable—from warm, to hot, to surface-of-the-sun—as Texas summers are wont to do. My routine solidified. There were those wonderful little trips on mass transit, during which I was oblivious to the pains of that dysfunctional southern public system. Those unnecessary hours waiting for a bus in the heat were still blissful moments for me amid what seemed a glorious jumble of experiences and new people. I made friends and settled into life in Dallas while living at home with my mother and her boyfriend. I had student loans and a low salary, so I paid what I could and helped however I could. But I could hardly begin to afford a place of my own.

Driven by my passion, I persisted with my plan.

I whittled down the suitability factors for partner countries and organizations. A partner needed to be founded and run by locals familiar with the community, registered with their local government, within two to three hours of the nearest international airport, and outside of war-torn areas. Unskilled volunteers could not provide the sort of advocacy, connection, or productive input if these necessary conditions weren't met, especially if they didn't feel safe. I investigated news reports and UN lists of organizations in or near cities in the countries that met the criteria. I called organizations in each country. One here. One there. As the months went on, these factors led me to narrow my search to NGO partners in four countries: Ethiopia, Tanzania, South Africa, and Ghana.

It's so strange now to think that anyone listened to me or corresponded with me at all. Some twenty-two-year-old kid from America calling and emailing them from a small NGO they'd never heard of. But they did listen.

Thinking back, I feel a bit ashamed. To my mind, it's a testament to the flaws of our economics that I, despite the hardships I'd endured and the hard work I'd brought to bear up to that point in my life, could so easily command the attention of these true leaders and heroes. The organizations I contacted were legitimate but small—they weren't in it for the money. Their employees' passions and selflessness dwarfed my own on that point. They served in the truest sense. Chalk up my ability to correspond with them to the privilege of being an American. Before the great recession. Before the pandemic. Before the erosion of American credibility. So call I did. Email I did. Until finally, I settled on two potential partners in the Ho region of Ghana, a few hours from the capital of Accra. This would be my next destination. Another journey.

CHAPTER FIVE

THE DiSaSTeR VOLUNTeeRS

My first impression of Ghana was muted. I arrived at night, and the airport was dark. Exhausted and already a full day behind schedule after issues with my flight, everything seemed to me green and dim. Yet, as always, in the deepest recesses of my very tired mind, there welled that excitement—the insatiable desire to explore what lies around every corner, to experience new sights, new smells, and to feel anew the energy of a people different from what I was accustomed to.

I had a small stipend of around $800 from my organization, and I had to make it last for my entire grand tour—not including lodging. And a grand tour it was, at least to my mind. I was now not only going to Ghana but also to Thailand and Laos to film and help assess the organization's volunteer programs in Bangkok and Luang Prabang. In total, my journey would last around two months. And the start of it all was here in Ghana. "The gateway to Africa," all the signs proclaimed as I waited for a taxi.

I don't know if it's meaningful, but for years I seemed to leave for big trips on rainy days and arrive where I'm headed in the depths of night. Whether it's a fact or simply a product of selective memory, that nighttime cab ride through a new city and landscape is now so familiar to me. Lights whirred by as we made our way into the city. I thought I could make out bright clothing in the darkness. I felt comforted by the unfamiliar; the beauty of a new place and its people was a distraction for my perpetually worried mind. I've always thought that it's a particularly human phenomenon to hold an optimistic view of human beings and to desire to know, see, and do more. As we drove exhaustedly through the crowded streets of Accra, my curiosity trumped my nervousness, my fear, and any thoughts of sleep or respite from a long flight seated next to wonderful but talkative neighbors.

My first destination was of a type that I would become very familiar with in my life: a hostel, this one situated in downtown Accra. It was the affordable option, given my small NGO budget. I'll never forget that, even in the dead of night, the hostel stood out as the brightest and most garishly lit place I've ever walked into or had to lay my head in. Bright fluorescent lights cast down onto starkly white minimalist spaces topped with raw wood. At the time, it was an aesthetic I found comforting, but my weary eyes reeled from the brightness.

"You are welcome," greeted the desk attendant.

I hadn't thanked her for anything. This would turn out to be a consistent cognitive challenge for me during my time in Ghana, a place where "You are welcome" is a literal statement of being welcomed into a place or space.

Looking back some thirteen years later, so many of those next twenty-four hours are a blur. I settled in and slept fitfully among a throng of bunk beds. The sun rose. I took an early morning walk through the streets of Accra. They pulsed with a unique energy. Something about them truly felt ... like home.

I met some of my heroes: the Disaster Volunteers of Ghana—or DIVOG. They arrived in a black van to pick me up from the hostel and take me to Ho, a couple of hours drive away through the countryside.

Today they call themselves Adanu. Though the name has changed, their mission has not. When I initially discovered DIVOG, I found their name strange. I thought they were a disaster relief organization. I was wrong. They worked to build schools and other facilities in rural Ghana to transform the lives of people in local communities. In their own words (and with their new name) on the Adanu.org home page:

> Adanu ignites the passion of Ghanaian communities to bring about a future filled with opportunity and hope. What we do at Adanu is quite simple:
>
> We build schools in rural Ghana using education to transform children's lives—and entire villages—forever. Adanu partners with communities to foster a spirit of collaboration and ownership. This creates authentic community development and true sustainability.

Every Adanu project is run jointly with local community leaders. This creates ownership, authentic community development and true sustainability.

A few young guys with initiative had created their own programs and processes to host volunteers and expose them to their community development work. So why that initial name: DIVOG?

Their executive director Richard Yinkah's words still ring in my mind to this day: "Every time a child cannot go to school, every time a family has no food to eat, it is a disaster."

In case it's still not yet clear, I'm a nerd who loves the futures depicted in science fiction—huge, grand, endlessly inspiring. To my mind, they all depend upon only one thing: the fuller realization of human potential. My travels may not have been among the stars, but at the core of my desire to work in development was that belief forged in front of the TV, watching Picard espouse the values and virtues the United Federation of Planets had achieved in maximizing human potential and building a better world where *anyone* had a chance at a fulfilling life. In that context, Richard Yinkah's words could not have been more profound to me.

I'm a nerd who loves the futures depicted in science fiction—huge, grand, endlessly inspiring. To my mind, they all depend upon only one thing: the fuller realization of human potential.

I spent over a week with the DIVOG team. I visited villages. I ate dinner with political representatives of the city of Ho. I ate fufu. I climbed Mount Afadja, the tallest mountain in Ghana, not far from the border with Togo. I listened to news reports about the construction of a new presidential palace and heard the debates. I saw the work that the DIVOG team did day in and day out. I was and remain humbled and inspired.

DIVOG wasn't the only organization I visited during my stay. I spent time with another organization in the Volta region that I had corresponded with before departing that oppressive Texas summertime heat. I sat in white plastic chairs in the centers of villages and listened as I was told of the need for additional wells for summer. I climbed other mountains. And I witnessed so many people doing incredible work.

All throughout, my self-doubt remained. Who was I to be "evaluating the fitness" of these organizations?

By the end of the visit, I'd cemented a partnership between DIVOG and my organization that would last about five years. Through our partnership, multiple schools would be constructed in the Volta region. Hundreds of volunteers would experience the programs and become advocates for the community. Many would be inspired, just as I was. Establishing that partnership remains one of my proudest achievements and is, to me, a testament to the power of passion and of volunteering.

I felt some self-doubt and some hesitancy at the thought of the outsized role Americans can play in the development process, but that hadn't stopped me from proceeding. It was strange to me that such amazing individuals and organizations would depend on small American NGOs with few resources and find the need to "pitch" themselves to US NGO staff members half their age with a tenth of their experience and knowledge (particularly about the problems in their local communities). Yet despite this, it was beyond question that my life felt just a bit more meaningful, any struggle just a bit more worth it. Actually, I was on top of the world.

CHAPTER SIX

LiTTLe DaiLy
DisasTers

My eyes were stinging. I had arrived in Bangkok from Accra by way of Milan and Frankfurt. It was July 2007. Thailand was blistering hot and undergoing a nontrivial amount of political upheaval at the time. Also, I had no clothes.

Well, that's probably a bit dramatic. I had the clothes on my body. I also had $500, what remained of my $800 stipend, and a few other possessions—a couple of notebooks, pamphlets, business cards—in a small saddlebag.

You see, my Alitalia flight connecting through Milan had been, well, exceptional. Imagine the shock of *every passenger* on the plane when we learned, after we touched down in Frankfurt, that the airline had not loaded a single bag before taking off. I recall being the lone American in a massive line of Italians and Germans, all screaming at airline staff (that last fact was comforting only in the sense that I could recognize it as a universally shared experience).

Mostly, I stood in shock.

I was three weeks into my two-month work trip. I had three objectives. First, to create the relationship needed for an African volunteer program in Ghana. Second, to offer on-the-ground feedback to programs in Thailand and Laos. And third, to film that promotional video as a tool to help increase volunteer engagement, particularly with the Southeast Asia programs. Standing in that slow-moving line of angry passengers at the airport in Frankfurt, that last objective felt impossible.

The camera equipment. All my clothes. My souvenirs, including the handwoven kente cloth I'd been given as a gift in Ghana. Gone. With only part of an $800 stipend, a little extra money from my meager salary, no credit cards (I didn't qualify for any of those until I was in my late twenties) to cover replacing the equipment or face any sort of emergency, the grim reality was that I could end up going halfway around the world to evaluate and film the Thailand and Laos programs and be completely unable to do the job. My stomach was on the floor. My pulse and my mind raced.

But hey, I'd craved adventure. I was committed to the work and to my passions. In that moment, standing in the middle of the Frankfurt airport, I distilled the chaos around me down to one simple choice. I could wait in Germany for my bag to catch up and, in the process, risk messing with a set of connections taking me to an appointment and a job halfway around the planet. Or I could board my connection and head to Bangkok to do the job I had committed to doing, the job I had dreamed of on all those morning commutes and during all those hours in the office, hoping my belongings, including the equipment I needed, would eventually catch up.

These are the kinds of choices that have defined my life: Either take a risk you never saw coming and shoot yourself off into an unknown void or shrink away. The result has been a life driven by an endless series of risks.

I decided to continue on. To take the leap. To have faith? I never put it in those terms—not until many years later. I took deep breaths and convinced myself this would be just a blip in my otherwise smooth travels. Little did I know the little daily catastrophes awaiting me in Southeast Asia.

I skipped across the world, stopping in Sri Lanka before landing in Bangkok. Once there, I found myself exhausted from the stress that naturally comes to those who hang out on limbs. As I roamed the avenues in Bangkok, a thick

THESE are THE KINDS OF CHOICES THAT HAVE DEFINED MY LIFE: EITHER TAKE A RISK YOU NEVER SAW COMING AND SHOOT YOURSELF OFF INTO AN UNKNOWN VOID OR SHRINK AWAY.

layer of pollution made my eyes sting and water. This was actually my second time in Thailand, having first come briefly three years earlier while on Semester at Sea. It was also my second time with limited funds and almost no possessions. The first time, my mentor Dr. James Evans, who was also serving as the dean of the ship, had personally given me the money I needed as I awaited the processing of my student loans and scholarships and the associated excess that I would be able to spend at my own discretion. This time it was just me. But there were aspects of

Bangkok that had a certain familiarity about them, and that familiarity helped to calm my nerves. Especially the smells.

I was ignorant of Thai food before I first set foot in Thailand. Growing up as a young Black kid in Texas with a single mother, it was not a part of my experience. But now, as I wandered through markets in the heat, the smell of the street foods—corn cakes, chicken on skewers, pad thai, and pad see ew, seemed to go on and on into delicious infinity. I know now that there's nothing like the ten billion different flavors in a Thai street market to explode my world. My mouth watered. Every step brought more temptation—temptation I had to resist, even while losing energy to the steam, the sun, and the humid air. I had limited funding, and thanks to my new favorite Italian airline, I had on this day a very special mission: acquire some clothes.

My bags would take at least four days to arrive at the airport. In that time, I had two days in Bangkok before being picked up by the organization's community partner and taken just outside the city to the site of that partner's programs. Once there, I would spend four or five days before heading north (my transportation not yet secured for that leg of the trip) to cross into Laos. Then, in Laos, I would volunteer, evaluate programs, and film other volunteers before heading back to Bangkok for a few days before flying home. In total I would spend about three weeks in the region. Me, a kid from South Dallas. Globe trekker. Exploring the world. I may have been without any of the things I needed, but I was still in heaven.

And what's the most fitting outfit to wear when it's hot and humid in heaven and you have no other clothes? White linen, of course.

The stall called to me. Linen pants. Linen T-shirts. Linen shorts. Linen button downs. I bought a couple of pairs of everything for thirty dollars or so. I was saved! A saved man of many linens. In case you're wondering, I wasn't concerned at all about that one pair of underwear I had in my possession. I felt certain it would all work out. I even had enough money left to get some corn cakes for dinner!

Returning to the hostel, I outfitted myself in my new regalia. It was only early evening, and I had another twenty-four hours yet before leaving the city. So I committed myself to go and do what has become, over the years, one of my sacred traditions.

When I first arrive in a new place, I take a walk. I walk with no destination. No objective. I simply walk.

As the temperature cooled and the sun began to set, I ventured out into the streets of Bangkok. It's a magical city of light and life. I walked and walked, lost deep in thought.

My mother was on my mind. Whenever I traveled, I was always excited to imagine showing her the places I had visited. Our relationship was always full of fun times, even when things grew difficult. She was a brilliant woman who sacrificed so much for me as I was growing up. She'd earned a full music scholarship and was among the first in my family to go to college. (I inherited her singing voice.) But she had traded a career as an opera singer for a career as a middle manager at Texas Instruments and later at Raytheon. She never blamed me for it or showed me anything but love. But even as a child, I heard her sometimes, overwhelmed and crying. A bill was late. She was lonely. Often, I would comfort her by making her laugh.

I imagined her with me wherever I went. Here in the streets of Bangkok. Earlier, in the jungles of Costa Rica or strolling through the temples of Kyoto or the insanity of Shanghai. She grew up singing choir, and once, listening to a local choir from Khayelitsha township in Cape Town, I wept to hear their beautiful voices, thinking about how she would have loved to hear them, to join them. And here in Bangkok, I knew she would love the food.

My mind also wandered to the work I needed to continue the next day. To operate effectively, I needed at least a little cash. Feeling rested the next morning, I set out to acquire some.

I don't know if you've ever heard any good stories about getting cash out of an ATM. If not, I'm honored to be the first to bring that excitement to your life.

I yawned. The heat, like the sun, was dawning, coming inevitably to sap my energy. In the back of my mind, I recalled my resolve to leave Texas and this kind of heat behind me the second I got a chance. Mind muddled with thick morning dew, I inserted my card into the machine and tapped in my PIN.

That's when I saw it, looming in the dawn light. *An elephant.* Sauntering down the sidewalk among the throngs of taxis and tuktuks. I turned in awe. I would later learn that it's illegal to have elephants walk the streets of Bangkok. As you might imagine, the impact of their feet on the pavement is terrible for them, and people end up hurt in car accidents navigating around them. I knew none of this. I had never seen an elephant framed by a skyscraper. In its way, it was beautiful.

I watched as the elephant passed, leaving behind the seeds of another day's little disaster.

As I turned to complete my transaction, the corner of my eye caught my card sliding with a whir back into the machine. I reached for it in panic. Too late. My cash was in the tray, but my card was gone. Like my luggage, it was now lost somewhere—in whatever ether exists within an ATM not attached to a bank, or between Milan and the far east. I now had fifty dollars cash in my hand, no card, and no way at all of accessing the rest of my stipend.

I lived my life wanting it to be a good story. Now I had a story about that time the elephant walked past the ATM.

Over the years I have had friends, fiancées, and girlfriends who either marvel at or become agitated by my penchant to remain almost robotically calm and rational in crisis situations or times of struggle. It's a trait I've come by after much practice. I may have felt fear, unease, and embarrassment, but I pushed down those feelings. I breathed deeply. Calmly and rationally, I started checking off the boxes marking transition moments in my travels.

Lost all the luggage you need to do a time-sensitive job halfway through a five-thousand-mile transnational flight? Check. Take a leap of faith that what you need will catch up and just keep going.

Stuck in a foreign country with no luggage or clothes except what you've got on your back? Check. Buy some linen from the street stall, clean your one pair of undies in the hotel tub, and keep going.

Stuck in a country with a job to do, no equipment, nothing but four days' worth of cheap linen clothes and one pair of underwear, fifty dollars to your name, and the need to survive for three weeks before securing transportation to yet another foreign land? Check.

Solve it.

I was exhausted, but I managed to use some of what little cash I had remaining to buy some time at an internet café so that I could find the right phone number for Bank of America. I called using a phone at the hostel.

A replacement card could be mailed but would take about a week to reach Thailand. In a week and a half, I would be in northern Thailand, about to cross over into Laos. I gave them the address of a hostel in the city in northern Thailand, Nong Khai, that seemed to have lots of availability. I hung up. Hung my head. And hoped. Surely it would all work out.

CHAPTER SEVEN

RESPITE

Thailand is beautiful. The traditional structures gleam. The only things brighter are the smiles on many of the people's faces. I was staying at "Mami's house." Mami ran an organization that had hosted hundreds of volunteers over the years. I was merely the latest to arrive.

The home was situated in a small village near a Buddhist temple, surrounded by lush green rice fields and forest. I settled into a quiet room and readied for dinner. I emerged to find a table brimming with colorful shared dishes.

Mami, her two assistants, and I ate together. They kindly repeated friendly warnings that the food was very spicy and might be too much for my feeble taste buds. Not all the warnings were heeded.

After three days of little disasters, I felt a calm sitting with them at that dinner table that completely altered my overall state. We talked about politics. Thailand's leader, Thaksin Shinawatra, had been forcibly deposed in a bloodless coup in September of 2006. Martial law had been declared in Bangkok and lasted into at least January of 2007. Just a few months before I had arrived, Thaksin and his entire political party had been banned. That bit of our conversation seemed muted, save the praise for the king and his family. It was a pattern I would notice daily during my time there, further exemplified by the ubiquitous royal family T-shirts.

We also talked about music. That topic has always helped me to connect with people across boundaries. After being prompted, I even sang a bit. As dusk set in, I feared briefly that the bug spray I'd been given to ward off mosquitos had tainted the food—the two things had started to smell the same to me. My hosts laughed as I learned that lemon grass—a staple of Thai cuisine—was also used to ward off bugs.

The next day, a full day ahead of schedule, my wayward luggage arrived from out the ether. Still penniless and clad in an all-linen look I'd grown fond of, I found myself able to breathe just a little easier. And able to work.

My first stop touring with Mami and her staff was the nearby temples of Ayutthaya. I wandered and took shots among the ruins, then set up a tripod and caught the visiting masses, marveling just as I was, at the stone giants. As Americans, we learn all about the architectural and cultural achievements of European civilizations, but almost nothing of Southeast Asia. The vast edifices stretching into the distance, topped by domed spires, were of a style different from anything I'd seen and a testament to the ingenuity and genius of people. I worked and wandered for hours.

Our next stop was an animal shelter. Mami's organization had taken on the task of helping to care for stray dogs, which had become a problem in and around Bangkok and surrounding communities. There were other volunteers here, so I took photos of them playing with the animals, helping to care for them by distributing supplies, and learning about the challenges they presented to communities.

There are certain breezes which seem to cool you at a defined pace and frequency; they have about them a steady rhythm. In just a few days' time, I had fallen into the soothing rhythm of exploration and work. I thought about how so many American and European expats go to Thailand. My interactions with them had not been pleasant, and I had already seen firsthand some of the less-than-upstanding reasons many are drawn to the country's beaches and brothels. But away from the boisterous madness of Bangkok, a moment in the green or on the beach had quickly made it clear why the nature of this place and its people can be so wonderfully alluring.

And then it was time to go.

I packed up my things. I bid my goodbyes. And I started my adventure anew from the platform of a train station in the heart of Bangkok.

I had about 536 miles and another border crossing to go and, still without my debit card to access the money remaining from my stipend, a little less than fifty dollars cash with which to do it. I guarded myself, keenly aware that I was one picked pocket away from being stuck in Thailand with no money to call for help, no understanding of the local language, and no way to get back home.

I first boarded the train to Nong Khai in northern Thailand. Luckily my spot in the sleep car was prepaid.

When I arrived, I hunted out the hostel to which I'd asked my card to be delivered. I'd found the hostel online before calling the bank: Mut Mee Garden Guest House. I walked from the station, suitcase and equipment in hand. I had not prebooked but was lucky enough to get a room.

I'd had a girlfriend in college whom I loved. She was an exchange student from Japan on the Pittsburgh at Bradford campus in northern Pennsylvania. The study-abroad office there had helped me get a Mitsubishi scholarship for summer language study, and so, knowing I was already fluent in Japanese, they called me in one day and asked me to meet her and guide her around campus. We fell in love. She was caring and beautiful and, to this day, the most selfless person I've ever met. We laughed for hours. I played guitar and sang to her my attempts at humorous improvised songs in Japanese. Our affection and passion for each other only grew over the months of her stay. At twenty-one, that had been my first experience of any kind of romantic love or passion.

The moment I locked eyes with the receptionist at Mut Mee Garden marked my second such experience. Even now, I'm not sure I've ever undergone a clearer realization in the instant of meeting someone that we would be engaging in more than just cursory small talk. She was here from Italy, traveling and working during a gap year. She was blond and petite, with a smile that distinctly reminded me of the actress Carey Mulligan playing Sally Sparrow in a *Doctor Who* episode I'd watched just a month or so before traveling ("Blink" is the episode name, for those of you who have not had the pleasure).

The receptionist told me there was no package waiting for me. My card had yet to arrive. She laughed at my elephant story and those bad Alitalia jokes I'd been working on for a week. We talked about music. She told me of a party happening that night on a small barge that waded out into the Mekong each evening. Of the drinks and good times that floated down the river. I was lost in her eyes, grinning ear to ear like a fool and standing in the way as others tried to check in.

I half forgot I was checking in to my own room. I even forgot that I get very nervous around women. Until I got to my room and put my bag down. I laughed at myself. There was no way I was going to that party.

I had a job to do. First things first, I needed to use some of my cash to call Bank of America and check on the status of my card. It must be arriving any day now, right?

"Just as a reminder, this call is recorded for training purposes," said a young-sounding man with a noticeably crisp American accent. Idle chit-chat and rote intake processes are so different when you're on the verge of being a homeless man halfway around the world—and being charged by the minute.

I spoke quickly but politely. "Yes, I'm just calling to check on the status of my card. I lost my previous card in Bangkok and asked for a new one to be expedited to my hotel in Nong Khai." I probably sounded goofy and happy from my earlier chemistry with the receptionist.

"Yes, just let me check on that for you."

Waiting. Grinning. Hey, she talked to me!

"It looks like your card was delivered!"

Relief. Deep breath.

"That's strange. I just checked in to the hotel and was told there was no package for me."

"I'm showing here that it arrived just this morning."

A sinking feeling.

"Can you confirm the address?"

"It was sent to your home address on Phoenix Drive in Dallas, Texas."

Heart on the floor.

"I don't understand. I made clear that I was in Bangkok and would need the card mailed to northern Thailand."

"Oh. I'm so sorry. I don't see a note of that. We can expedite you another card to your location? Can I have the address? It'll take just four or five days."

Some part of me broke. I thought to myself, this happened because I got happy, because I'd felt content for a moment. I hadn't been vigilant.

THAT PESSIMISM WAS, AND REMAINS, PERPETUALLY AT ODDS WITH MY PASSION, MY DESIRE TO FOLLOW THROUGH ON A MISSION, TO ALWAYS HAVE A STRONG VISION FOR A BETTER WORLD AND A CLEAR MISSION TO MATCH.

That kind of pessimism had usually kept me on my toes, much as it also weighed heavily on my heart. Over time, I'd learned to be skeptical of anything good in my life and to double down on dubious inspection of anything delightful. That pessimism was, and remains, perpetually at odds with my passion, my desire to follow through on a mission, to always have a strong vision for a better world and a clear mission to match. More often than not, though, the force of that passion pulls me past my darkest moments and my deepest skepticism.

But first, I needed to consider my rather limited options. I was once again at a crossroads, my own annoying "choose your own adventure" book. I had to continue on my journey, up through Vientiane and on to Luang Prabang in Laos, which included:

- Paying for at least one night at the hotel (ten dollars)

- Crossing the border from Thailand into Laos. For this, I would need to pay for a visa before crossing (thirty dollars)

- Getting transportation from Vientiane to Luang Prabang (at least ten dollars)

- Eating (at least fifteen dollars)

I had grown accustomed to eating only once a day, so I could perhaps make all this happen for sixty dollars. I had thirty dollars. And I needed to arrive at my next destination in two days.

Longer-term solutions screamed in my mind as tears welled up:

"Make more money, you loser."

"Find out how to get a damned credit card."

None of it was helpful in the moment. I thanked the bank representative. I hung up. I put my head in my hands. I breathed.

I'll figure something out.

The sun began to set. Dusk was settling in. I grew up in a city. I had just come from Bangkok. By contrast, this place was so quiet.

Here I was, doing things that my mother, and others in my family, could not even imagine. Surely, I could solve the issue of needing money to keep traveling. I left the lights off as the sun went down, alone with my thoughts in the dark. I could reach out to my boss, the executive director. She had always believed in me and trusted me. But I was afraid. Afraid that she might then think that I was not able to do the job. My mother and my family couldn't help me. My mom barely made rent the month before I left. Memories came to me of my aunt and mother sending money I needed when I was perpetually destitute in college. But now in Thailand?

Let me tell you this: if you're ever stuck somewhere in the world low on cash, with no way to access funds in your account, and without a credit card for payment, know that it is still possible to get money to yourself. Here's my advice.

First, always have your bank account and routing numbers.

I did not. But I made a gamble. Took another leap of faith after talking to the world's loveliest hotel front desk attendant. I walked through town to the nearest internet café, and I made a bet with 10 percent of all the money I had in the world. I purchased thirty minutes at a computer, logged in to Bank of America, checked my current balance, and found my account and routing numbers. I had thirty minutes, so I rushed, writing the numbers down on a notepad in the garish light.

Second, remember that Western Union and MoneyGram exist and will wire almost anywhere in the world. It just costs a lot to do it.

I'd hatched this plot as I sat in the dark in my hotel room, head in my hands. It should work. I had just never done it before.

Third, remember that there are apps for that.

It's odd to think it now, but in 2007, the iPhone had just come on the market, and the internet still moved like molasses at the best of times.

I went to Western Union's website and fiddled around. Every minute felt like an eternity. I didn't have even a dollar to waste. I could not find what I needed fast enough. And then I did. I entered my bank account information, and with just a few of my thirty minutes left to spare, I wired every penny in my account to myself, minus a massive 10 percent transfer fee. I was no longer on the verge of being homeless in a foreign country! I was about to have almost $500 to my name!

I walked out of the café breathing heavily. The cash would be available for pickup tomorrow, unless something else happened, some other problem to sort out. I stood against a wall and cried a bit—a mix of anxiety and relief, despair and hope.

I would deal with the rest of it tomorrow. Tonight, I needed a drink. And I knew just where to get it and who to get it with.

The barge took off for its first trip around 8:00 p.m. I left half my cash hidden in my room and took with me the other half, about fifteen dollars.

The Mekong is huge, and on this night, the river was calm. The boat was full of young people: a German philosophy student who liked shots of tequila as much as me; an American "dude bro" with his girlfriend; a teacher from Japan who introduced me to the concept of the Round-the-World airline ticket and who would be in Dallas in just a couple of months. Faces from all over the world, and there in the corner, a pair of eyes that constantly met mine. Lingering looks, flips of the hair, small movements of the shoulders.

I was out of my depth.

Increasingly drunk on tequila, I picked up a guitar as we made our first of two trips back to shore. I played a song I had written. It was called "Through the Seasons," and it was a song that manifests all the feelings instilled in me by my favorite poem, "Fancy," by Keats.

Ever let the Fancy roam,
Pleasure never is at home:
At a touch sweet Pleasure melteth,
Like to bubbles when rain pelteth;
Then let winged Fancy wander
Through the thought still spread beyond her:
Open wide the mind's cage-door,
She'll dart forth, and cloudward soar.
O sweet Fancy! let her loose;
Summer's joys are spoilt by use,
And the enjoying of the Spring
Fades as does its blossoming;
Autumn's red-lipp'd fruitage too,
Blushing through the mist and dew,
Cloys with tasting: What do then?

Sit thee by the ingle, when
The sear faggot blazes bright,
Spirit of a winter's night;
When the soundless earth is muffled,
And the caked snow is shuffled
From the ploughboy's heavy shoon;
When the Night doth meet the Noon
In a dark conspiracy
To banish Even from her sky.

It's a poem that has become part of my philosophy of life: a belief that without winter there can be no enjoyment of spring, without hardship no true joy in success. It's a philosophy that helps me find some joy in times of struggle. And in that moment, singing it helped me feel a sense of contentment believing that without my little daily disasters there could be no moments like this. Floating along the Mekong, I felt contentment. In a foreign place and with a group of people I couldn't have put together even in dreams, I sang, I received applause, and I felt tranquil. As the barge docked, I saw her stepping off. My heart sank just a little. My inner monologue lashed at my insecurities.

Why didn't you talk to her again?

I don't even know her.

All you had to do was go up to her!

It was too hard.

I stayed aboard the barge, growing tired but wanting to squeeze just a little more out of a night I felt sure I'd remember forever.

As we prepared for one last trip down the river, she jumped back aboard. That's when my courage got the best of me.

We talked all through the night—on the ship; in hammocks on a patio attached to her room, looking out across the river; in bed, sleeping in each other's arms. She was only the second person I had ever been with.

She was beautiful in the morning light. I got her Myspace account. I packed up and said goodbye. I would never see her again, but at least I had been right about that night.

Walking again through Nong Khai in the early morning, I was relieved that my earlier gambit had paid off. I departed for Laos the next day, cash successfully in hand.

I arrived in Luang Prabang ready to work. The ancient capital of Laos was stunning. Every morning, Buddhist monks walked through the streets collecting offerings. Men and women on scooters held umbrellas to shield themselves from the midday sun. Cafés lined the streets along the Mekong. The night market was a place full of wonder and Luang Prabang was itself a place full of people with a kind of quiet solemnity and a place of worship that seemed to permeate everyday affairs.

While on site, my expenses were covered by my organization and our partner in the city. Another volunteer and I built a washroom facility for a local orphanage. I had never worked so hard, mixing cement for ten hours on several days, laying the foundation for what the organization hoped would be a more suitable station for the children to wash up. I worked, and I filmed the work. I caught video of the city and of the monks.

In all, those months passed in a blur. I breathed deeply, and just as quickly as I exhaled, I was home again in Dallas.

CHAPTER EIGHT

Mission Accomplished

I've come to believe there are people for whom work is what they do so that they can live their lives, and then there are those who live their work. I've never believed that there is one right way. But I have my way.

Maybe I'm the classic INTJ on the Myers-Briggs test, moving through life as if it's a giant chess board. I *never* just do a job (and now I make it a point to not support hiring anyone for my team who just wants to do a job). Every task is a problem about which to strategize. Every day is an opportunity to find a better solution to that problem and to move on to a new problem. I even find myself imagining whether a problem even is a problem and become actively indignant at problems that just shouldn't be problems. I do everything I can to ensure any mistakes never manifest again. I don't just work. I embark on missions.

When I began at the NGO in Dallas, I was excited to work on international volunteerism. And my experiences profoundly changed me. For one, I began to see that I could handle myself in a crisis. My confidence in that realm might even have gone too far. I believed I could find some way through any problem. It was just a matter of time and careful consideration.

I had also come to admire the people I'd encountered while traveling: US diplomats, UN officials, and NGO and aid workers. Being a foreign service officer or similar institutional actor remained a dream, but my mind had opened to new movements and methods that might positively shape and change how we improve the state of the world and relations between peoples. I came to believe, and still believe, that international volunteering is a practice at the heart of grassroots international development and global advocacy. Much like grassroots volunteer work in the United States and elsewhere, it is defined by a process of democratizing involvement of ordinary citizens in the solving of bigger-picture problems and the achievement of larger goals.

We can even see examples of this dynamic in our local communities. Volunteers wander through hospitals singing carols to raise the spirits of the sick and the dying. Ordinary citizens are mobilized to provide assistance to underserved and under-resourced neighborhoods in their communities. Temporary staff and volunteers who may know little of local ordinances show up to help us manage vital election processes. International volunteerism is this same activity on a global scale.

When it comes to volunteerism as a tool for advocacy, I have argued that as more of us better understand the true state of the world, we can make a more effective case—to our congresswoman, to our MP, to any of our leaders—that they should not cut development budgets but rather expand them to bring to bear even more human ingenuity and resources to improve the state of our world. In this way, international volunteerism—done right—means that ordinary citizens around the world—from north to south, south to north, from east to west and west to east (when done right, there is movement in all directions)—can be involved in advocating for and driving change. In effect, international volunteerism is a means for involving the entirety of humanity in the future of humanity. In my opinion, it is not just an option; it's a requirement for a better future.

INTERNATIONAL VOLUNTEERISM IS A MEANS FOR INVOLVING THE ENTIRETY OF HUMANITY IN THE FUTURE OF HUMANITY.

I am also emboldened by one thought: no endeavor with *only* state support persists or is successful in the long run. There will be no ultimate success if only the technocrats, even with their vast expertise, are invested in moving us forward. Public involvement is the seed of real change, particularly in democracies.

When I began my mission and set out on my journey eastward, all this had been in my mind as I'd approached my three goals:

1. To start the organization's first program on the African continent

2. To visit and report back on conditions encountered by volunteers

3. To film a promotional piece for the organization's work

I brought my passion to this work, along with the hope that I would gain additional international experience. I learned more about program management and coordination. I built my expertise in international development and foreign policy.

Now I was back. With that mission completed, I sat each day in that same sun-filled room looking out over that manicured lawn, overwhelmed by restless impulses and discontent. It had been nine months since this journey began, since I had first walked nervously through that big gate, across the gravel, and into that small home office in Dallas. I had grown.

Richard from DIVOG visited to finalize our program agreement. Our organization would send volunteers to Ghana who would pay a fee for housing, transportation, and food on-site. The logistics would be handled by DIVOG, and a percentage of all fees would go to each organization, theirs and ours. DIVOG would be free to develop relationships with volunteers who visited, helping to fundraise and create stakeholders who cared deeply about the communities they were exposed to. We agreed that the partnership would last for about five years.

My only remaining task was to edit and complete the video. I pieced together scenes from the world I had come to know in my two months of travel. Monks among the temples of Thailand. Volunteers mixing cement in Laos. The team in Ghana smiling, volunteers carrying foods from farm to local food banks. I spliced in other footage I'd taken previously while on location as an intern in Costa Rica, scenes of beautiful waterfalls and volunteers experiencing the life of people in a small town in the mountains—milking cows, making cheese. To this day I'm amazed that it's watchable. But I think it is (and not just because I'm in half the shots).[2] All that work. All my

2   You can judge the finished product for yourself: https://www.youtube.com/watch?v=FPlJSBPFiWl

experiences. Everything boiled down to this two-minute promotional video backed by the music of Sigur Rós. Watching it today, I'm still driven almost to tears by the memories it calls up. The stress of having no money or resources or fallback plan in a foreign land. The joy of finding innovative ways just *to be* and to work. Memories of struggling to do it all with an eye always on my future. All that is wrapped up in every frame I see.

I also see the faces of people who have deeply inspired me, like Richard, or the organization's executive director, who always placed faith in my ability to accomplish things beyond my years. I see myself mixing concrete and smiling, standing amid nature's majesty; I see myself wandering ruins and finding a romantic spark along the Mekong.

And I remember distinctly that when I arrived back in Dallas, that green lawn outside my office looked different—*felt smaller*. I had brought my passion into my work, taking every opportunity to strategically use skills that applied to jobs I wanted in the future. I had a plan and vision: The Foreign Service, the UN. I had felt that I was on my way! It was late 2007, and my only question was: what will be my next challenge?

CHAPTER NINE

I'm a Producer

Among my most vivid memories is sitting in the car with my mother some early mornings on the drive to school or on holidays or weekends to run errands, a concept that has faded in a digital world. From the car radio would come a flow of sounds that invariably left me quiet and awestruck: NPR. The voice of Diane Rehm. The daily updates on *Morning Edition*. Nothing calmed me more. I learned as much from NPR and PBS, and specifically from its North Texas edition KERA, as I have ever learned from any school. My mind and attention were always rapt and reveling in the worlds painted by the distinct style of reporting that's made that media organization famous.

I have yet to be as nervous as I was the day I interviewed to become a production assistant at its KERA studios. Walking through uptown Dallas in late fall in my hand-me-down double-breasted pinstripe suit, I was comforted by the thought that no one would know that my dress shoes had sizable holes.

Uptown Dallas was at the time the most walkable area of the city. All around were new condo buildings and high rises, extending the footprint of "urban Dallas." Yet its skinny and empty sidewalks provided none of the energy I remembered from my travels, the stuff that called forth the curiosity that eclipsed my nervousness and exhaustion. Instead, I walked through uptown Dallas in the early morning on legs of jelly, passing glass skyscrapers until I arrived at the KERA studios, a lonely lot on a hill. I had applied for the production assistant position on a whim. And now here I was, arriving for my third and final interview.

I took the job and started work in January 2008.

In some ways 2008 was the best year of my life. In other ways it was the worst year of my life. Kind of like the season-three intro of *Babylon 5*, the one where they intone: "It was our last, best hope for peace. It failed."

Or maybe it was more like the Charles Dickens classic: "It was the best of times, it was the worst of times …"

I lean toward the former, with the modification: "It was my last, best hope for some stability. It failed."

Things started out well and then got bad. I know now, looking back, that they could have been much worse.

Right then, in January, Lehman Brothers was still a thing. Housing prices seemed as if they were going to rise forever. Millennials like me were struggling to get jobs, but that was probably because we were "the worst." Gen X was jealous that we wouldn't settle for paying ten years' penance to squeeze two ounces of opportunity from a saltshaker like they had. And boomers were mad because we worked with headphones on (I could never determine another reason).

I was hired as a production assistant for *Think*, a public affairs talk show in Dallas. I'd loved the show for years. I'd even edited my video while spending hours listening to archived episodes of host Krys Boyd asking insightful questions live on air. In my new role, I screened calls from the call-ins, recorded the show, and edited out the breaks to produce the podcast. I called and confirmed booked guests the day before and coordinated their arrival. It was simple and straightforward.

It was also exciting.

One of my first days on the job, we interviewed General John Abizaid, a commander of US forces in Iraq. I met David Frum, now with *The Atlantic*. Though I'm about as liberal as they come, Frum's interview made me a fan, and I remain one to this day.

I was in the studio every day with amazing minds.

From the day I took the job, I also introduced myself to anyone who asked as the assistant producer rather than the production assistant. At first, I did this unintentionally. I was shaking someone's hand, and the words just fell out. They felt more natural. To this day I don't know how it was perceived. But I persisted. Soon enough others were referring to me by that title too.

In all honesty, although changing my title had occurred that first time "in the moment," it was also the product of my mild obsession with job titles. Not only did I know, for example, that I wanted to be a diplomat or development officer, but I also knew that I wanted titles like Deputy Chief of Party, Country Analyst, or Foreign Service Officer. Those titles served as ominous standards—anything less distinguished loomed as a mark of failure. Looking back on my ambition for high-ranking titles, it's hard not to conclude now that job titles, especially the ones one comes across early in one's career, are much less valuable than the experiences that help you explore the life you want.

Comfortable with my self-bestowed title at KERA, I began a process of looking beyond titles and breaking down my roles to an inspiring description of a set of functions. I started asking myself:

What do I *do* in my role? And what about that action or function do I *find appealing*?

In this case? There was a lot to enjoy, but there was nothing I loved more than *being around some of the world's most powerful thinkers and ideas.*

I shook hands and talked fast food with Morgan Spurlock, director of *Super Size Me*.

I got free tickets to endless performances.

I met and spoke to Sir Ken Robinson shortly after his viral TED video, screened questions for him on the show, and then went to his lecture later that night at the Dallas Museum of Art.

JOB TiTLes, especiaLLy THe ones one comes across earLy in one's career, are mucH Less VaLuaBLe THan THe experiences THaT HeLP you expLore THe Life you want.

I met MacArthur genius award winners, a UN undersecretary general, Pulitzer Prize winners, Nobel laureates.

I also made good friends, some of the best coworkers I've ever had.

I was twenty-three and living the life in early 2008.

I was in a state of constant nerd-gasm as *The Dark Knight* and *Iron Man* topped the box office.

Racism was dead.

Obama was about to be elected president.

I made $15 an hour and moved into my own apartment.

I even got a date or two.

I felt rich on my $30,000 salary and right at home in my native Dallas, land of roaming leased BMWs.

I was ballin'.

CHAPTER TEN

Man, The Economy is Bad for Everyone else

What I remember from 2008 is the feeling of a world that was starting to crack and crumble into a million pieces. The evidence of impending disaster was piling up around a lot of us.

My mother had been struggling with rent for a while. Then she lost her job. I tried to help, but I only had so much to give. Things seemed to get worse when she and her boyfriend, Edward, moved to the suburbs to get a cheaper place. She'd made too much money to qualify for a federal housing voucher, even though now she was making no money.

My best friend from college and "adopted brother" Will Kim had moved to San Francisco after leaving Pittsburgh. We'd bonded, as two adult only children with struggling single parents do. He's half Taiwanese, half Korean. We came from different places, but we understood each other's struggles. The California dream had always been his dream—surf, sun, and freedom. But there weren't many jobs for graphic designers in San Francisco in 2008. Will worked odd jobs as prices for housing, food, and just about everything around him became more and more unimaginable.

Other family members of mine had trouble getting to work. Gas had gotten so expensive.

There were public voices that strove to calmly and rationally explain why our economy was shifting beneath our feet.

George Bush said things on TV.

Hank Paulson said things on TV.

I fell in love with Kai Ryssdal and *Marketplace*, especially the sound of his brave attempts to explain how everything around us could simply collapse.

All those voices were powerless to stop what came. The market crashed.

All around us, the world that we had taken for granted was falling to pieces. In the chaos, and as a new graduate still just starting to think about my place in the world, I did what I could to grab my little piece of what remained.

I had my first livable salary and my first apartment: a little one-bedroom unit on Gaston Avenue near downtown Dallas. I was five blocks from the lowest tip of the Greenville Avenue neighborhood, one of the most vibrant in the city. I had a local bar (something I now consider an essential feature of any good neighborhood). The world may have been going to hell in a handbasket, but I, with my usual singular focus, was taking the next step in my continuing quest for urbanity. I continued to revel in that glorious distraction of walking the busy avenues of a big city. That was the life for me.

I bought a couple of guitars from a local pawnshop. For a couple hundred dollars, I scored a Gibson ES 335 copy that still retailed for almost a thousand dollars and also picked up a Stratocaster in mint condition. People were pawning all kinds of amazing things. Brand-new things! I didn't think too deeply about why at the time, but nowadays I'll go to pawnshops to gauge the coming status of the economy. When the volume of nice, shiny, new things exponentially increases in a pawnshop, things overall might be on the verge of getting very bad.

With my new guitars, I spent time cultivating my love of singing and music (this includes a love for karaoke that has annoyed every partner I've had to this day). I'd take my new guitars into one of the KERA studios on weekend mornings to record some of my songs using the station's sound equipment. Sunlight would shine through windows onto the white sound board, and I'd fancy myself a real musician. I even started to put a little album together under the name "Verdant." It featured "Through the Seasons," that song from the barge on the Mekong, along with other pieces I'd written.

One bright spring day, I came home from one such session and found my mother sitting at my place, slowly and somewhat secretly sipping on a shot of cheap flavored tequila I'd bought. I'd been in the habit of having only one shot to pregame before going to a party, so I'd been wondering for weeks on end why the bottle was getting emptier and emptier. Pleased to know I wasn't losing my mind, I laughed and joined her. We got tipsy, opened all the blinds and windows to let in the spring light and air. We listened to my music together. She cried and said that she was proud.

I put a little band together, and we gigged on weekends at bars in Deep Ellum, the center of the live music scene in Dallas. Half the people in the audience insisted that I write some originals and not just play covers of Tracy Chapman songs. I laughed and sipped my beer. We played no Tracy Chapman songs.

Briefly, I dated my neighbor. She was a model who was a full six inches taller than me and terrifying. By "terrifying," I mean that I quite literally was convinced that she was going to harm me in an Ikea during a dispute about Swedish pronunciations and meatballs.

Overall, I was happy, even as everything from economists' growth projections to unemployment numbers were flipping all the way upside down. Every day I woke up and thought: "Wow, things are really getting hard for a lot of people out there."

We OFTen joke THAT, in America, everyone THinks THey'LL BE riCH one Day. BUT THere's anoTHer, more insiDious siDe To American exceptionalism— everyone THinks THeir struggLe WiLL never come.

We often joke that, in America, everyone thinks they'll be rich one day. But there's another, more insidious side to American exceptionalism—everyone thinks their struggle will never come. Yet it does. Hard times come for nearly everyone. They'd come to my mother. They were coming to others around me, despite the pretty posts on social media. There's a line delivered by the character Andy Bernard in the series finale of *The Office*, "I wish there was a way to know you're in the good old days before you've actually left them." Looking back, I wish I had thought about how my own struggles, too, would come.

CHAPTER ELEVEN

HOPE AND CHANGE?

"**T**hank you for calling *THINK*. This is Brandolon. What's your question?" I asked politely.

"Hi. I have a question for your guest," a woman drawled back with a very strong Texas accent.

For those of you who are unfamiliar, a Texas accent is not a southern accent. It's difficult to describe precisely how it's different, but it's actually quite different. I hear it as a little faster, a little more curt, a little more passive-aggressive than the rest of what constitutes "the South." You'd not mistake it for anything heard in *Gone with the Wind* or other glorified depictions of southern patricians on their stately plantations.

"Of course, ma'am. What's your question?" Best to respond with a *ma'am* in these situations.

"Well, you see, I just heard your guest say a few minutes ago that Obama is Black. I keep hearing this and seeing this on TV, and I'm just curious why, because he's mixed."

I seethed. In about six months on the job, this was perhaps the hundredth time I'd gotten this "question." As is my habit when agitated, I looked around, trying to ground myself in the context of my environment before responding.

My colleague was manning the soundboard. My senior producer was sitting next to me, reading the newspaper and preparing both for the next hour and for tomorrow's shows. In the next room, through a pane of glass, the host had her headphones on and was deep in conversation with our guest. I breathed.

"Well, ma'am, Obama calls himself a Black man, and so I think that's a big part of the reason that you've heard that language," I responded calmly. Heads in the studio turned in curiosity.

I'd sometimes have to step out on occasions like this one, and when I did, I would often come back to find my replacement fielding an agitated caller. I might be full of passion, but I'm generally always calm. That said, no one had ever yelled at me. Until now.

"But he's a mixed man, half white, and grew up in Hawaii!"

I heard you the first time, lady, I thought to myself.

"I'm just a big supporter of Obama, and I think that people need to be reminded that he's mixed. I just don't understand why they don't say that!"

"I'm sorry, ma'am. May I put you on hold?" I replied through gritted teeth.

In these moments, what would flash in my mind is every news report I'd ever seen about a dark-skinned man. *The suspect was a*

Black male. The suspect is wanted on suspicion of . . . Their faces—often shown utterly dehumanized, their names left out—would be frozen in a graphic on the top right- or left-hand corner of the screen. I don't remember these reports ever attempting a nuanced examination of the ethnic heritage of the Black "suspect" in question. I could not for the life of me recall any discussion of where said suspect was born and raised, or of what that might mean for how we, the public, should perceive them. No. To me, the conclusion to be drawn from all this was both disturbing and nauseating.

Did anyone give a damn if the suspected criminal on the evening news is referred to as Black, even if they're half white and from Hawaii? We accept the designation of a Black male suspect, but let that same Black male do something good or achieve others' respect and a modicum of power and suddenly you find yourself fielding endless requests to clarify how they're actually not Black, but instead half white and from Hawaii. I stared into the distance. I pondered. This question had already been answered on the show, and I had only my little slice of editorial power to exercise in response.

I never took her off hold.

The 2008 election was a singular moment. But then, history is filled with singular moments. It seems that about every five to ten years, some big happening enters the collective consciousness. Over the course of a lifetime, there are probably no more than a dozen of these "collective moments" that anyone of a general age or generation can together remember as if they were yesterday. As I see it, this theory cascades down to smaller and smaller scales. There are singular moments for your city, your friend group, your relationship life.

2008 was full of those moments for me.

When Obama took the stage to great applause at the Democratic National Convention, when he stood and claimed leadership of the party, my every bone trembled. There was a knot in my belly when I produced the station's live election-night coverage. Hundreds of thousands listened as we interviewed pundits, tracked the polls. And in the moment that we knew Obama had won, I was in disbelief. He had won despite the obvious racial obstacles to his election, obstacles I had seen manifest in all the calls from listeners contending, "He's not Black! He's mixed!"

Later that evening when, to the enormous crowd gathered in Chicago, Obama gave an acceptance speech filled with gratitude, kindness, and hope for what we all could achieve, I fell to the floor of my small apartment in tears. It still felt surreal. It was a moment that fundamentally altered what I thought was possible. He looked like me. He looked like dudes in my family, in my neighborhood. He made it cool to be a calm, intelligent Black man.

Surreal as it was, that was also a moment of hope for me. I believed in what we all could achieve if we were all empowered. And I knew I wasn't alone in being filled with that sense of hope and optimism. An entire generation of millennials looked out at a world turning sour and saw a glimmer of hope that the fundamental structure of our society and the way we view ourselves within it could be changed for the better.

I WANTED TO BE A PART OF THAT CHANGE, PART OF MOVING TOWARD THAT VISION OF A WORLD WHERE WE ALL HAVE THE FREEDOM TO BREATHE AND TO DREAM.

I wanted to be a part of that change, part of moving toward that vision of a world where we all have the freedom to breathe and to dream. Watching Obama speak to America that night, I grew more excited at the possibilities of that future and my potential place in it.

It's hard to think now of that night kneeling in front of the TV being the moment at which the fictional worlds that occupied my imagination in my youth—those better places—seemed more possible than ever before.

That's because despite the election of a Black man to the presidency of the United States of America, the world—at large and at home—had a different idea.

Lehman Brothers collapsed.

Everything around us was clouded with doubt and the endless consequences of bad debt.

And a recession that had looked bad for everyone else finally began to touch me—a gentle tap at first and then an ever darkening and forceful embrace.

I had just gotten a raise. I was only just beginning to conceive of a life. I'd made so much progress. But I feared being laid off. How would I help my mother with rent? How would I pay my student loans? What if there was a gap in my resume? Moving up any further or getting any substantive pay increase now seemed entirely out of the question.

I felt that I was falling behind, that what little I'd attained for myself was precariously balanced on a knife's edge. I had to take another step forward. Another leap of faith. Another risk.

CHAPTER TWELVE

THe Exam anD
THe EYEPaTCH

Every year, about twenty thousand people take the first steps toward becoming a foreign service officer. These individuals are the foundation of the work of the US State Department. They are US diplomats stationed in our consulates and embassies abroad. 45–50 percent of applicants clear the first hurdle, the foreign service officer test. Of those who pass, 25 percent also pass the Qualification Evaluation Panel. All who are left are invited to go to Washington, DC, for the final test, a full-day oral examination. In the end, maybe five hundred to seven hundred applicants, 3–5 percent, pass the final test and receive an offer to join the Foreign Service. Those who enter do so in different tracks as economic officers, political officers, public affairs officers, and on. Given my experience in media and partnerships, I had chosen the public affairs track.

I sat in a nondescript office building in Dallas with the test, that first hurdle, before me. I sat and clicked through a long multiple-choice quiz of questions on economics, politics, history, pop culture. For years, I'd been so nervous about taking it. It was easy.

After passing, I also succeeded in the qualifications review and was invited to Foggy Bottom in DC to sit through the day-long interviews.

I love Washington, DC. It is my favorite city in the world. My mother brought me for the first time when I was about thirteen. I was on spring break, and she had a work meeting. We stepped onto the metro, and I remember feeling that we were in a real city! I'd never left the South before that trip. Subway systems and public transportation used by people of all stripes, creeds, colors? That was stuff from movies about New York and London.

Our first stop in DC proper was the Smithsonian station. DC is not cold, but to me at thirteen, having never left Texas, I might as well have been in the Arctic. I could feel the chill the moment we stepped off the train. I marveled at the high concrete vaults of the station. It was like a cave from the future built by a super-advanced civilization. We rode up the escalator, out of the dark and into—snow! White, fluffy snow fell onto us as we emerged, landing on and covering everything in sight.

I looked to the right, and there was the Capitol building—the very one I'd seen over and over again on our TV screen during PBS's *NewsHour* with Jim Lehrer. Here was the real thing. I looked to my left, and there was the Washington Monument, jutting up from white earth. The sun stood watch behind it, guarded by a thin cloud cover.

And in front of us, a band! A quartet was playing Canon in D directly opposite a group of protesters. Just out of the subway station, we were already surrounded by these marvels, along with throngs of tourists out strolling even in the cold.

My mother and I would later recount it as our best trip as a family.

Now, years later, I was set to venture back in pursuit of my dreams. We both knew how much it meant for me to make this trip. I could never forget the look of pride on her face the morning I departed. I was so close to achieving my next big goal.

"You're working at the embassy in Germany," my questioner began. We were in a small room with a small window—an arrangement that seemed to scream bureaucracy. I don't know how many opportunities I'll have in life to be interviewed and questioned intensely by someone with an eyepatch. But I can say that I've done it once. Despite my nerves, I did well.

"You've just gotten word that a passenger plane full of American citizens has just crashed on the tarmac in Berlin," she continued. "What do you do?"

"I contact the ambassador to inform them of the accident and cc any other relevant staff to open lines of communication for a response. I also assess the damage. How many people were on board? How many of them were citizens?"

"You hear from a source that there were sixty Americans on board," she said, continuing the scenario without hesitation.

"I communicate a rough number to my team and to anyone that needs to know. I also reach out to local and American media outlets. They may learn facts before I am able to, including a more accurate count."

"You find out that a story is going to be run that will question the safety of American-manufactured planes."

"Well, I've been in contact with the media, so I reach out to understand why that angle is being taken. I confer with the team. I argue that the focus for now should be on the lives lost. There aren't enough facts yet about the incident."

So it went. Back and forth. On and on. I sat there for almost an hour, feeling more and more emboldened. As I answered each question, I noticed that the next question pertained to information I had covered in previous answers, giving me the opportunity to build on earlier actions. I was steps and steps ahead. *Isn't that a big part of leadership?* I thought to myself. I had never felt that way before about my abilities.

Another exercise involved working together with other applicants. We were given a single budget and set of projects, and we had to make a case for which deserved funding. In presenting my project, my breath caught. I literally choked, and the world seemed to come to a stop. Time stood still for me as it has on only a few occasions in my life. Time slowed down so much that I had plenty of time, in the space of a thought, to engage in my usual dance of self-confidence and self-doubt. I mentally lashed myself and called myself a loser. My mind raced. I knew the stakes, and so after what may have been a two-second pause and what felt like an eternity, I recovered and finished making my case. Recognizing fully in that split second that I was not making my absolute best case for my project, I pivoted and made a strategic decision to argue for another project, minimizing the spending of my own but offering ways that it could be effective if built over time in phases.

There was an essay. Then other challenges.

At the end of the day, all of us, several dozen, sat in a room awaiting results. They called people to leave the room one by one. Until there were about eight of us left.

My eye-patched interrogator opened the door somewhat gingerly and strolled into the room. The eight of us had passed.

It wasn't until a few hours later, back at the home of a friend who was letting me crash, that the magnitude of it hit me.

I'd struggled just to be able to go to college in Pennsylvania. Unable to afford flying every trip between home and campus required arduous forty-plus-hour trips on a Greyhound. Even those bus trips, though, were often beyond what I could afford. I'd spent endless hours alone on campus during holidays— alone for Thanksgivings, Christmases, and spring breaks. Then, after graduating, while I'd occupied myself with my mission and my ambition, there was a constant and endless game of juggling student loans and trying to help with my mother's rent.

THIS WAS WHERE IT ALL HAD LED. ALL THAT WEIGHT LIFTED, AS IF SHACKLES HAD BEEN REMOVED. I FELT AS IF MY HEAD WAS EMERGING, SCREAMING, FROM OUT OF A DEEP FOG.

I lay there at my friend's house, reflecting. This was where it all had led. All that weight lifted, as if shackles had been removed. I felt as if my head was emerging, screaming, from out of a deep fog.

It was the first time that I would come to truly understand the close relationship between economic opportunity and a concept we all take for granted.

Freedom.

I wept for hours.

CHAPTER THIRTEEN

THE WAIT

What happens to a dream deferred?
Does it dry up
like a raisin in the sun?
[...]
Or does it explode?

Langston Hughes pondered this question in his 1951 poem "Harlem." But I have had occasion to ponder the question myself. One conclusion I have reached is that a dream deferred is approximately one hundred medium-sized one-topping Domino's pizzas. And yes—they do dry up.

I drew this conclusion because that's about how many pizzas I ate in the winter of 2008 and early 2009 as I waited for my clearances. I dreamed of foreign deployments and new adventures (this time without the specter of poverty). I thought about having a salary of over $50K that would allow me to pay my student loans. I'd be rich! I would be able to help my mother and perhaps even my extended family. All my passion and ambition had led to this point.

I had international experience, specifically experience in the development space, and experience creating marketing and promotional materials as well as managing partnerships. I'd negotiated cross-cultural agreements. I'd been a radio producer. I had a BA in communications. I had prepared myself to make an excellent public affairs officer at a US embassy.

That my dream of stability might actually be achievable was a thought I'd never had before. I started spending hours online looking at apartments in DC, the buildings where I'd be trained, and reading about the lives of foreign service officers engaged in the important work of negotiating treaties, creating cultural exchange programs, facilitating foreign aid, and making other changes that could create ripples of positive energy through entire economies. Some of those officers could even afford to have drivers! I couldn't even afford my own used car if I'd wanted one.

These weren't the only new thoughts. Even as I boarded the plane from DC back to Dallas, grinning ear to ear (I had passed!), I looked around and felt a feeling that was new to me. I saw older passengers, children accompanied by caring parents stowing their luggage, all without a care in the world. I was seized by an overwhelming pride that I would be part of the shield that helps to protect all of them. A foreign service officer. A diplomat. Securing peace and positive relations with America's allies.

I was energized.

There were a lot of next steps. But I took on all of them with glee.

With limited health insurance, I visited a free clinic to get my medical clearance.

I had my Japanese.language abilities tested in a call with the Foreign Service Institute. Possessing that ability boosted my pay level.

I talked with the FBI investigator working on my security clearance at the central public library in downtown Dallas.

Had I smoked weed? Yes, once.

Why was I late on my student loan payment? I had to help my mother with rent.

Had I ever been treated for mental health issues? Yes, I'd made a few visits to the free services at my university when I was a freshman. It was harder than I thought adjusting to being so far from home and so alone. (I left out the part where my depression became so crippling, I spent three days lying in the dark listening to Bill Withers's "Ain't No Sunshine" on repeat, unable even to check email. It didn't bear mentioning. It was a long time ago.)

I'd traveled a great deal, and I was told they would have to interview others I'd met. My ex in Japan called to tell me the FBI had come by her home to interview her. My friend and informally adopted brother, Will, in San Francisco got a visit. My mother too.

I joined a Yahoo message board for others who had passed the exam. They shared stories and asked questions about everything from pay scales to the joys and pitfalls that could be expected from specific deployments. It was a heady time. I was giddy with excitement.

I waited.

A month. Then two. And then three.

I pride myself on being patient and calm and always acting rationally. Yet during these months, I came to know anxiety in a new way. As that anxiety—along with sadness and fear of failure—grew, so did my belly. I'd always been thin and fit, but I gained ten pounds in those few months as the bright horizon turned dark and ominous. Unable to muster the energy to cook, still struggling under a mountain of juggled bills I could barely afford to pay, I ordered cheap pizza after cheap pizza. Consequences to my health be damned.

Still I waited. I longed for the final decision, for that stability to come to my world. While I waited, the world around me continued to go to shit.

It was late 2008. I had my own apartment now, but in the heat and humidity of a long North Texas summer, my mother's AC had stopped working. The landlord refused to fix it. He wanted everyone out so that he could refurbish the place.

WHILE WE ALL STRUGGLED, WE WATCHED ON THE NIGHTLY NEWS AS BIG BANKS THAT FAILED GOT DEBTS REDUCED OR ELIMINATED. THEY WERE BAILED OUT WHILE WE WATCHED, POWERLESS.

My mother, once a contract negotiator on a decent salary with Texas Instruments and Raytheon, had finally found a job as a debt collector with MBNA/Bank of America. The job paid almost nothing. The healthcare was terrible. She couldn't afford a move, and I couldn't help her.

Together, we learned that we weren't alone. She would come over some nights, and we'd occasionally pour some boxed wine or some of that cheap tequila. She would tell me the stories of all the ordinary people she would call who couldn't pay their bills. All the people making daily choices between groceries, student loans, and revolving debts. All the people forced to take out payday loans that backfired. People who couldn't pay their mortgages and were losing their homes. They were all making the same kinds of choices we were being forced to make. Debt collectors called to tell us we were all failures. We deserved no sympathy. Yet while we all struggled, we watched on the nightly news as big banks that failed got debts reduced or eliminated. They were bailed out while we watched, powerless.

I knew I wasn't waiting alone for those better times to come, but every day that I waited for my dream made the entire national spectacle a more bitter pill to swallow.

CHAPTER FOURTEEN

I can HeLP

That bitter pill was even harder to swallow in my work.

Every day saw an endless parade of guests and listeners coming into the studio or calling in to the show to talk about the bailout, the recession, economic stimulus, tax cuts, layoffs. It was an inescapable topic and a constant reminder of everything that can go wrong, all the fears and economic anxiety that can be realized.

It was so hard to live inside of these conversations when my own growing fears and anxieties haunted me the moment I woke and followed me deep into dreams each night.

I waited.

I was told the clearance had been known in some cases to take up to a year and a half or even longer. With each passing day, I felt more and more certain about one thing: I did not want to be the person who observes and reports on the news, the person who produces a show featuring guests who bring amazing ideas to the public—guests who change the world.

I knew the immense value of what we were producing. Shows just like ours had transformed my childhood—indeed, my entire life. I understood that this work could change the world. Yet I felt more certain than ever that I wanted to *make* the news, to have *my* ideas heard. I realized that I wanted to be one of those world-changing guests on the show. In hindsight, I see that this was one more step along a path that moved beyond my limited understanding of social impact. I was slowly shifting from a single-minded focus on a small set of jobs, titles, and careers that I thought could change the world to a broader view of the many ways available to us to change things for the better, and the many choices we have regarding which methods we choose.

> I WAS SLOWLY SHiFTiNG TO a BROaDER VieW OF THE manY WaYS aVaiLaBLE TO US TO CHanGe THiNGS FOR THE BeTTeR, anD THE manY CHOiCeS We HaVe ReGaRDiNG WHiCH meTHODS We CHOOSe.

So after only one year, I left the world of NPR and my role as a producer with KERA to return to the NGO I had worked with out of college. I clung to my core beliefs, my driving insights, and the purpose to which I had committed myself. While I was newly enthralled by the thought of finding new ways to make a difference and have my ideas heard, I figured that if I was going to wait to learn the outcome of my clearance, at least I could more directly help others in the meantime.

It won't surprise you that I leaped into the work.

I revamped the organization's orientation and training materials and procedures. I was able to convince the executive director to hire my adopted brother, Will, to do graphic design and layouts. It was dawning on me that we had to do everything we could to support the opportunities of people in our circles and in our community.

I traveled to Jamaica to evaluate the program there and retrain the volunteer coordinator within our community partner (in the process, my count of marijuana experiences may have surpassed one).

The coordinator was consistently at least an hour late to every appointment with our volunteers. It was something I had to see to believe. And see and believe I did. I convinced him that even if we accepted that he was on "Jamaica time," as he insisted, the volunteers he was educating and shepherding through this new culture and experience were not. His persistent lateness, without context or explanation, stood in contrast to the substantive sacrifices of time and money the volunteers had made to be present and to achieve some good. His habit seemed to me callous. Worse, it was slowly closing the volunteers' eyes and ears to learning more about the culture. They needed to be met partway.

He didn't listen and was sadly the first person in my career that I would ever advocate to be let go.

I represented the organization on a commission at the Brookings Institution called the Building Bridges Coalition. It was an initiative promoting US "soft power" through the Peace Corps and international volunteering. So many of the Coalition's views—including that international volunteering was a valuable diplomatic tool to positively change perceptions of the United States and build more stable relationships with allies—echoed the conclusions I'd reached in my first stint with the organization. I dove into the dialogue and even wrote a radio op-ed on the topic that aired on my old station.[3]

I felt newly committed to work, the meaning of which was palpable. I felt relief no longer just listening to others talk about their ideas and the work they were doing. I could instead directly measure my own impact. How many schools were built? How many volunteers became donors? There was some peace in that, but still a specter loomed.

I waited.

One more month went by. Then three. Then six. I waited through the seasons as winter 2008 turned to spring and then summer 2009.

I don't like waiting. It can be excruciating and deflating as all the initial enthusiasm and vigor slowly fades away.

I watched on social media as others who'd passed the exams along with me posted about their deployments. I watched my friends live lives that, through the lens of Facebook, seemed so perfect: new jobs, new relationships, new travels (with associated photo albums), and new adventures.

I ordered Domino's pizzas.

Eight months passed. Then ten. A year. 2009 became 2010.

I remained in that same urban cabin I'd arrived at just after college, looking out on that same green grass and graveled driveway. I longed to move to some next step, some new place. Instead, I was stalled.

It's true that I felt some satisfaction each day with the knowledge that I was directly helping others. Thoughts of my prior travels also helped when the wait grew dark. I reminded myself that I had already been places I would never have dreamed I'd go, places some people never see in their entire lifetimes. I reminded myself that I was

---

3   If you're interested, it's at https://www.keranews.org/texas-
     news/2009-05-15/commentary-global-volunteerism. The audio is lost to
     time, but the transcript remains.

only twenty-four years old. Sometimes nothing is more reasonably grounding and sobering than a productive comparison of oneself to the mean. I found those points of solace to keep me afloat as I waited on that next step into the Foreign Service.

All this was peppered with a bit of denial about my actual circumstances and a strong desire to make my mother proud.

Surely there was just a bureaucratic reason for the wait.

I grew dreadlocks and doubled down on my music hobby. My band got our best gig at this time, playing originals and a couple of Bob Marley covers on the rooftop of a downtown bar. On a cool summer night, we stood on stage to a crowd of dozens, making music framed by the Dallas skyline.

Anxious and depressed about the job I awaited, I nevertheless couldn't help but fully commit to the job I had. I won an award for my work, an "ExxonMobil Community Champion Award for Nonprofit Work."

I resolved to help other kids like me, kids who might never see the world outside of their hometown, who might otherwise never have the chance to reap the benefits I had reaped from international travel. I wanted others to have their own adventures.

So I convinced my executive director to start the "Global Wings Scholarship." I coordinated everything. I found a local partner to screen disadvantaged high school students from around the area. I raised the scholarship money online and through a raffle. I recruited volunteers. I partnered with the Marcus Graham Project, then a nascent operation aimed at helping young African American students find careers in the advertising industry, to create promotional materials. I planned their destination (our Costa Rica program) and itineraries that involved, among other things, helping local environmentalists protect struggling sea life along the beaches.

While outwardly it may have seemed that I was driven by confidence, ambition, and purpose and that I was achieving something worthwhile, inside I felt my usual self-doubt growing. I struggled to sleep for fear of what news of my own failure tomorrow might bring. And as the sun rose, my tired eyes would open to new days where the fear of failure and an overwhelming confusion almost kept me from getting out of bed.

The program was successful. We sent three students to Costa Rica. They referenced the experience on their college resumes, and one of them got into and has since graduated Harvard. In dark times, it was one of my brightest moments, but any feelings of success were fleeting.

Scarcity is cruel to the mind and body. I was still making only fifteen dollars an hour. My mother still couldn't move or pay her rent, and I could barely pay my own. I was once again mired in forbearance on my student loans. The feelings of failure, confusion, and disappointment were inescapable. Social media made it all worse. Every day I felt as if my heart were in a vise. And every day it felt as if the fetters—maybe a bit loosened and almost slipped when I'd felt that hope after passing the exams?—were being refastened. The wait was a darkness, my efforts at good works the only light. It was a pattern that persisted paycheck to paycheck, week to week.

I waited.

Thirteen months. Fourteen months.

Finally, I heard.

I had not received a "suitability clearance." In other words, I was told that other officers had judged me unsuitable to be their colleague. I was told I had too much student loan debt.

My education, the very thing that had put me in a position to hope for the best, now had seemingly robbed me of that hope. High debts and a salary too low to properly address them while also supporting my mother—these details had now blocked my path. I'd clung to roles that paid less, because I believed that the work was valuable, that my ambition to do socially good work despite its low pay showed character and a commitment to principles. Now I couldn't help but feel that all of it made me seem like no more than a fool.

I appealed. My mentors and coworkers all wrote letters on my behalf testifying to my character. All of it was to no avail. I didn't even know I lived in a country where it was possible to be turned down for this work because of debt.

My dream was dead. And there weren't any other jobs to be had. I was stuck. I was broke. More than that, I was broken.

CHAPTER FIFTEEN

Dreams in the Ashes of Dreams

I would like to say I've conquered sadness and depression. But I suppose one can't ever really say that. Emotions can't—and perhaps shouldn't—be conquered. The Vulcans, cyborgs, and androids in sci-fi TV shows and movies might have that ability, but not real live human beings.

It had been six years since I'd received that scholarship to travel as part of Semester at Sea. A world that had seemed so small and cruel to me had burst open on that trip. I learned what an NGO was. I'd opened a pamphlet given to me by a foreign service officer in

Venezuela and saw for the first time that there were possibilities that I had never known for who I could become.

I would often think even farther back, to how far I had come from being a rebellious kid. I had leapt into the ether, all for a dream.

A dream I thought I had achieved!

Just the promise of a livable wage and healthcare through the US Foreign Service had helped me feel a kind of freedom. It was a sense of freedom I may not have known at all if I had not had this opportunity to feel it, even if only temporarily.

Now that feeling of freedom had disappeared for a reason I did not fully understand. Once again, each day returned to being only another day in which to be concerned about the financial problems of tomorrow. I felt as if the shackles were back on my wrists. I couldn't go on thinking that the daily struggle just to live, let alone the struggle to hold on to dreams in the face of adversity, was just the nature of life. I became more keenly aware of what I didn't have.

The experience of being turned down at that final step in the process led me to interrogate my circumstances and to see them as part of a larger structural problem. The world's inequalities now seemed more acutely a problem to be solved rather than a fact to be accepted. I had tasted the hope of something better. I had realized how little it might take to remove so much of the worry from my day-to-day life.

And so, I went about life at that point full of conflicting emotions—saddened by the loss of a dream but fueled as much by anger as by that drive I'd always felt to take something and make it better.

It was 2010. The waiting, the stress, the complete inability to support my mother had all created a little circular patch of gray hair on a straight drive north from the tip of my nose. I was prematurely gray, a very old twenty-four.

Dallas, Texas, has never felt like home. Texas, to me, is a place dominated by stereotypes and their corresponding expectations. Growing up, there seemed to me to be little room for people or things that are, or desire to be, different from some role they've been designated by the little world around them. Dallas, in particular, seemed always striving to be something it was not.

Its admittedly beautiful skyline soars above the great plains. Stately glass towers outlined in neon lights suggest a similarly towering cosmopolitan energy. Yet the streets below are empty, devoid of life. There are high-class restaurants only miles from the nearly burned-out ruins of neighborhoods which define South Dallas, where I grew up, or the area around Fair Park, where the Texas State Fair is held annually. The city even built its own bridges to nowhere, a stunning design from world-renowned architect Santiago Calatrava that was meant to invigorate a city-wide revitalization project called the Trinity River Park. The park would have been one of the largest urban parks in North America. But it was embroiled in a decades-long controversy because the city wanted to build a highway through it. The park debacle modeled the city's inner tensions, like that beautiful bridge over a ditch into a neighborhood that would have loved any genuine physical connection meant to stimulate economic growth and opportunity. But the entire affair was nothing more than an exercise in vanity for a city where style can too often eclipse substance.

Surely no place is monolithic, I told myself. *I could build a life here.*

To start, I could stop sitting on my couch in the dark ordering cheap pizzas and waiting for a better future.

I got on OkCupid. I reached out to old friends. I made it a goal to surround myself with people who I felt were true gems. Feeling robbed of dreams and any sense of choice when it came to my career path, I found a new solace in art and design and the many choices, the freedoms, that creativity can be a testament to. I started going to small gallery openings (with free champagne!). I took walks past old mansions down stately Swiss Avenue and tried to imagine what was still largely inconceivable to me—the lives of the people who lived there.

I threw karaoke parties in my apartment and became a regular at a local bar called Zubar. I would walk in and, before even sitting down, there would be a cider and a shot of tequila waiting for me. I talked for hours with the bartenders. Every Tuesday, I would stop in to get lost to the tunes of CoLab, the house band.

And much of the same solace I found in art I increasingly found in music. I would sit at home and listen for hours. I developed an obsession with the Canadian band Metric, which eventually turned into a love of electropop. I finished my own album from the tracks I'd recorded in the station's studio and enjoyed with my mother.[4] I played open mics around town, sat in on sets with rappers, and fell in love with Deep Ellum and the Dallas music scene. After being knocked for a loop by my long wait, I worked hard to make Dallas my home and set myself on solid ground.

Of all the things I'd tried, I'd never been to a music festival. So when a friend invited me to a "Homegrown Festival" in a new park in the heart of downtown Dallas, I couldn't resist. It was a beautiful summer day. Music from two stages situated on opposite sides of the park reverberated off the windows and walls of the urban forest. Food trucks, stalls, and vendors lined the edges. Texas-standard advertisements for Tito's and Shiner Bock called out through bold, big banners and a giant blow-up beer bottle.

---

4   Here's the link if you'd like to check it out: https://www.reverbnation.com/brandolonbarnett. The first song there is "Through the Seasons," the one I played on the barge in Thailand. Some of the others, like "Wanted & Free," capture exactly how I felt at this time.

Homegrown Festival on the day I met Messay

There are a few things I unequivocally love about Texas. The low cost of getting drunk, or at least extremely tipsy, the barbeque (specifically the brisket), the Tex-Mex, and the opportunity to talk and lie in the grass as live music washed over me.

"I think I've seen that girl before," I said to my friend as we stood in line for some cheap Shiners.

"Which one?" he asked.

"Over there. She's Ethiopian. I think that's the girl I've been talking to on OkCupid."

"You should go talk to her."

My pickup lines at the time ranged from "Hey, you look bored" to "You're very pretty," followed by awkward grinning. I was not smooth. It was also ninety-five degrees that day and humid. My primary focus was on getting a cold beer and finding a place to sit and enjoy the music. And what if I only *thought* she was the woman I'd been corresponding with? I could end up approaching a strange woman, staring deep into her eyes while saying hello, only to experience the embarrassment of learning that she had no idea who I was. Wouldn't that be great? I'd have a lovely new memory of being the awkward creep at my first music festival.

On top of all that, I didn't even know her name.

"What am I supposed to say? 'Hi, are you brewhaha? I'm musicman69'?" I responded.[5]

"You could leave out the terrible screennames. But yeah. Just say 'Hi.' Maybe sing her a song."

"Very funny."

Despite all my doubts, I was tempted—not to sing her a song, but to say hello. Because what if it *was* her, and I said nothing? We had been corresponding for two months already, writing long messages to one another on everything from politics to OkCupid's racial dating research. My interactions with her were among the only times I'd really smiled over the past few months.

"Fine," I acquiesced, as we inched forward in line. "But first I'll need a shot. Maybe two."

"Sure. I'll do them with you. Although I feel like we were gonna do that anyway."

"Hmm, you're probably right."

Shots in belly and Shiner in hand (I'd like to suggest some iteration of this as a viable candidate for a Texan mantra, perhaps replace "shots" with "brisket"), I approached her. She was of average height, thin, with long curly black hair and caramel skin. She stood with another woman, shorter, also seemingly Ethiopian or East African.

---

5   These were not our actual online names.

I grew even more nervous as I drew nearer. Some of my Shiner spilled onto my shoes, a small and insignificant detail amplified in my mind by the moment of panic it induced. Had they seen? No. I was one among thousands. Only I was aware of my bungling and the trajectory of terror it signified.

She smiled and laughed loudly, lost in her conversation. Already, she seemed to embody the genuineness and light-heartedness I would expect of the woman whose messages I'd eagerly anticipated for months. In that smile and laugh, I saw hints of the other traits I'd come to admire: genuine curiosity, an open mind, and a kindness and optimism grown and nurtured in a world beyond the experiences I'd known. She'd grown up in Ethiopia and had emigrated to the United States when she was about twelve years old. Her family had been through a lot, but her parents and extended family, with a strength that comes from unity of action and purpose, had helped to shield her from some of the blows that poverty had dealt me and my single mom. She was not privileged, but also not scarred in the ways I felt I had been. She also had a more straightforward view of the world: less frustrated by endless unsatisfied ambitions and more fulfilled by those daily treasures I so often took (and still often take) for granted when they came my way—time with friends and family, enjoying the love of others.

"Hi. I'm sorry to bother, but are you boohooawful? I'm musicman69. I think we've been talking on OkCupid?" My friend was right. I should not have led with the names. My day was ruined. No amount of shots was going to make me forget this feeling of being mortified. Now even the music would be ruined.

"Oh my god. I am?" The reply was awkward.

"Sorry, I know the name is stupid," I replied with an equally awkward laugh. "I'm Brandolon." I reached out my hand.

"It's nice to meet you in person," she said with some shyness, as she took my hand in hers. "I'm Messay."

I consoled myself that this was not a case of mistaken identity.

"This is my sister," she replied. We shook hands. I signaled for my friend to join. The four of us settled into the festival. As we spoke, I was as enraptured by Messay in person as I'd been in our messages. A feeling of warmth and homeyness welled up in me as we all sat in the grass and talked with the sounds of a band called "This Will Destroy You" in the background.

I would see her again a few days later. We met at the Balcony Club, a jazz club in East Dallas near where I lived. It was and remains to this day one of those places where you can't be sure if it attracts an older clientele or if everyone there, from the house bands to the bartenders and customers, has been coming there so long they've aged right alongside the venue itself. She walked in wearing a black summer dress; stunning.

I came to see that through all the feeling of loss and the goals and dreams that I continued to hold on to, I was really seeking my own freedom.

My time with Messay reinvigorated me. I came to realize that my ideals had butted heads against my needs. I came to see that through all the feeling of loss and the goals and dreams that I continued to hold on to, I was really seeking my own freedom: the economic freedom that I now understood all people needed for a better future, the freedom that would enable my ideas and voice to be heard and have impact, the freedom to do work that improved lives. I realized I wanted to feel at least somewhat unburdened by fears of failure, by the weight of unpaid debts, unburdened from the misery of feeling guilty about spending money on a nice meal or a concert.

As Messay and I explored art galleries, new restaurants and bars, festivals, and museums together, the tension between my needs and ideals seized me even more. I had struggled to rebuild my foundation after what felt like the loss of my only chance at escaping poverty and achieving my dreams. But at the same time, I felt that I had become complacent, that I was standing still.

Something had to change. I needed a different job from my work at the NGO, and I needed a new dream—one that would allow me to better balance these two competing urges to do good and to feel ... free.

That was easier said than done. Unemployment was around 10 percent. Of my friends who had jobs, none of them seemed to be doing anything they actually wanted to do. Every international development job I applied to in Washington, DC, seemed to want me to live there before finding a job (something I couldn't afford to do) or to have a master's degree. There seemed no place for me to go except back to school.

The economist John Maynard Keynes has been one of my heroes since I first read him as a high school senior. From the moment I'd been exposed to it, his approach to economics struck me as logical, empathetic, practical, and elegant. I was struck by the massive impact his ideas had on our world and found it easy to connect Keynes's theories to the stories that my grandmother had told us of her childhood during the Great Depression. So it was that, in considering graduate schools, the one place that occupied a special place in my imagination was the University of London School of Economics, the very place where Keynes had developed many of his ideas. I also greatly admired a man named Basil Davidson, a scholar at the University of London

School of Oriental and African Studies (eventually the school's name was officially changed to SOAS). The sights in Japan and elsewhere in the world during my Semester at Sea had inspired me in college by instilling in me a craving for more knowledge of my own history. In those moments, his work had taught me more about African history and culture than anything else I'd been exposed to. London to me was thus a dreamland, a home of grand, world-changing ideas and inspiring characters (including everyone from Winston Churchill to the fictional Doctor in *Doctor Who*).

The programs there were also substantially cheaper than American graduate schools, while being of equal quality for my field of study. Most importantly, I would get to embark on a new adventure.

I applied on a whim the summer of 2010 and was accepted for a master's in international studies and diplomacy at the University of London School of Oriental and African Studies.

Maybe I could build something new after my dream had crumbled to pieces? Stability and its many little freedoms still alluded me. I had a new path and a new adventure laid out before me. It was June, and I'd be living in London come August. There was just that one familiar obstacle: I was broke.

I laid out a plan to save the funds I would need to survive in London. It all hinged on four months of personal austerity and student money that remained for my discretionary use once my tuition and fees were paid.

Then, as fate would have it, I was laid off.

The NGO I was working for depended upon paying international volunteers to sustain its social impact model. As the economy worsened, the number of people that could pay for flights and the number of donations to cover lodging, staff time, and other costs plummeted. The organization was too small to pay unemployment benefits. To get by, I withdrew the thousand or so dollars in my 401(k). It was not enough. With two months left before starting graduate school, I had no job and a decimated plan.

I was also in love.

Messay and I talked constantly. The more I got to know her, the more enthralled I was. She came to my band's performances, sitting in graciously rapt attention on rooftops around Dallas and dive bars like The Bone. We stayed awake for hours learning each other's favorite things, and we continued to write seven-hundred-word messages back and forth, expressing what felt like the entire spectrum of human emotion. In just a few short months, it had become difficult, if not impossible, to imagine a day without her.

She was dealing with her own stresses from the tanked economy. She'd gotten a music scholarship and graduated with an accounting and English degree from Southern Methodist University, gotten a job at one of the big-four firms, and then, like many, found herself laid off as the recession picked up steam. She also harbored a deep and abiding love for classical music.

We learned so much from each other.

That summer together, I'd begun a long process of learning from her different ways of managing financial affairs and understanding my financial worth. Whereas I'd focused on my finances only to the extent that they impeded or empowered my dreams, she was attuned to the value of saving as an investment in one's future. From me, Messay learned the beauty and power of finding ways to connect your passions to your day job. She'd been feeling stuck in a role as a financial advisor (after a stint as an audit consultant), but through me she more fully embraced the very love of the arts that had gotten her a full music scholarship to SMU. Soon after being laid off, she took a role as an accountant with an arts organization, the Dallas Black Dance Theatre, one of the most successful modern dance companies in the world.

From one another, we acquired tools that were essential to our aspirations. I was reshaping my dream by seeking a graduate degree. She was exploring an equally deep yearning to change lives through the arts, as hers had been changed when she first arrived in the United States at twelve years old and was handed a violin—an instrument which became nothing less than a sturdy lifeboat on a turbulent sea—before she even knew the English word for it.

Together, we surveyed my options. I could pretend to be able to save enough to live for three months or more in London until my student loan funds arrived. Or I could cast aside my pride in a way I had never been capable of doing. I could move beyond the shame I felt, like back when I had risked being stranded penniless in Southeast Asia, and I could really and truly ask for help.

The year was 2010. Online fundraising was nascent, and crowd-funding was at best in its infancy. I sent notes to family members, to Dr. James Evans, the dean at my university, old coworkers and profes-sors, and anyone who I thought had found reason over the years to believe I was worth something.

In an economic downturn, it's very easy to believe that you're worth nothing. The thought haunted me without mercy as I pushed Send on every request. When I wasn't spending time with Messay, I sat alone in the dark for a day, two days, waiting to hear back, waiting for all the noes to flood into my inbox.

One by one, responses came pouring in. $500 here. $1,000 there. My mother, who was still struggling, gave me all that she had and committed to sending me anything she could every month. The woman I was madly in love with, who'd known me only a sliver longer than two months, wrote me a check for several thousand dollars despite her own struggles. My mentor Dr. Evans and his wife, also a professor at Pitt, pitched in as well. When all was said and done, I'd raised around $6,000 to get me through my first months in London. Others' generosity touched me deeply. I hadn't realized how much I needed external proof that there were people in the world who believed I was a worthy investment.

I pawned everything I had, including multiple guitars I'd been able to acquire over the seven or eight years since I started college. The rest I would have to figure out on the ground. I said my bittersweet goodbyes and left behind everything I'd become familiar with, the life I'd started to mold for myself over the last three years. Now all that was left was to make myself and others proud.

CHAPTER SIXTEEN

Long-Distance Love and That London Hostel Life

I arrived at Heathrow in the dead of night on a rainy Tuesday. I couldn't resist the allure of a classic London cab. It was to be my last indulgence for many months.

Sounds of club music emanated from the youth hostel near Russell Square. It was the only remotely affordable lodging I was able to find near campus, and it was a haven for gap-year students as well as a seemingly endless supply of people visiting London solely to hang out in clubs. Who was I to judge? I'd have joined them if I'd had the money.

Instead I crawled into my bed, one top bunk in a room for six. I was thrilled at the prospect of renewed adventure and sensed that the next morning would cast light on a whole new world for me. At the same time, there was that bleak recognition of the gamble I'd taken once again. London is expensive. Would my limited funds last until my student loan payment came through? Would the student loan funding last until I got a tax return and then another disbursement? Could I find a job quickly? Accepting the obvious principle that I could not stay in hostels forever, there was also the essential question of where I was going to live.

The thrill of adventure superseded all my concerns. I smiled in anticipation and nodded off to sleep.

I woke to find a London that was both less and more than I had imagined. As is my custom, I walked and walked for hours, past the campuses of Russell Square, past the British Museum. Turning here and there, down mews and alleyways. As the day wore on, crowds appeared, drinking pints just outside the pubs. Kings Cross towered over me, and cobblestone streets stretched out below.

London felt unique among all the places I'd visited. It was a place where the old and the new intermingled in such a way as to produce a palpable tension, the kind that might come from witnessing a modern electropop group perform live in an old and stately museum. There was an overwhelming cosmopolitan energy throughout the whole city. With every corner I turned, I also realized another significant feature: I was not visiting this place. For the foreseeable future, this city would be my home.

My first days were a blur: orientations, new student mixers, my housing search. I would return each evening to the hostel, having spent as much time away as I possibly could, to sit in the lounge amid the thumping of the piped-in EDM music. It was the only spot in the place with reliable Wi-Fi. I sat there, resolving life crises as everyone around me discussed in a rainbow of languages what clubs or bars they'd visit that evening. I'd lose myself in apartment listings—all of them homes in neighborhoods I didn't know. Their details referenced tube lines and stations that were alien to me. And all of them were priced obscenely. Rooms barely large enough for a bed were renting for three to four hundred pounds a month, around six or seven hundred dollars at the time. A king's ransom for someone on the knife's edge.

Day after day, my search continued. I fell into a pattern: I would find a potential listing on Craigslist or the University's sites. I would reach out to the point of contact and arrange a viewing. I would hop on the tube that same day or the following day. And, almost without fail, either before departing or as I was arriving, I would receive an email or text on my new, cheap UK-compatible phone that the place had been taken.

One month went by, then two, then three.

In classes, I was surrounded by beautiful minds and ideas. Engaging was not a matter of choice; getting an education had never felt so thrilling. Messay and I wrote and spoke over Skype daily. And there was the beauty of the city, each day being unveiled to reveal new details.

I had my joys.

Yet I could not avoid falling deeper into despair. If freedom was what my heart longed for, this didn't feel like it. I moved from one hostel to the next each week, each one more affordable than the last, and each farther from campus and the heart of the city. Just as in the past, when I'd found myself making choices between food and rent, or student loans and my commute, here, too, I found myself making similar calculations. My funds were running out, and even once-a-day meals at McDonald's and local fish and chip shops were only delaying the inevitable. My mother sent me money every month, as much as she could, to help me stay afloat. Even with her help, if I could not find a place to live soon, I would need to return home and consign myself to another dream deferred.

"You're welcome to come live with us if you ever need a place."

We were standing at a bus stop. He was one of my classmates. Older, wearing glasses and a cardigan, with kind eyes and a wonderful British accent. I would have pegged him as a serious scholar even just passing him on the street. "My wife and I have an extra bunk in our living room. There are already two others living with us."

"I'll definitely think about that," I replied, with no intention of giving the proposal serious consideration.

I wanted my own space to breathe.

A few days went by, then weeks.

"If you all still have that bed available, I'd love to take it."

Little did I know the joys that moving in would bring me. The cast of characters in my life grew suddenly and exponentially.

There was Peter, a classmate in my program, who ran a local nonprofit and dreamed of international crisis management work. He was one of the most politically passionate individuals I'd ever met— and still is. His hunger for service was irrepressible. We would talk endlessly about transatlantic politics. Peter introduced me to scotch on my birthday (creating a lifetime love) and will always hold a special place in my heart for the manner in which he seemed to approach everything in life—with a thoughtful patience that transcended any I've seen. My only gripe with Peter was his woeful understanding of the full breadth of diversity within American cuisine. Jambalaya alone, after all, should be considered a global treasure.

Then there was Lilly, Peter's wife. She was a primary care physician. She had just finished medical school and had taken a break to stay home and raise her and Peter's first child. I'm sure that raising a one-year-old with four grown men loafing around your two-bedroom flat is not easy. Yet Lilly was so clearly focused. Her strength seemed to me unceasing.

Their child, Abraham, was the first one-year-old I'd ever lived with. I watched him grow into his terrible twos, climbing to higher and higher perches and taking more and more risks. I couldn't help but find myself bemused at his attempts to get to the highest bunk. Wasn't I doing a different version of the same? Trying to climb higher and higher and take on more and more risk?

Next was Zack. At the time, Zack was an assistant to the archbishop of Canterbury. He had a collection of board games in the flat that not only expanded my mind but also saved me a lot of money; for months I was able to join board game nights in lieu of nights out on the town.

Then there was Charles, who became a close friend and confidant and was the most unwitting "playa" I've ever seen. He was French, in his midthirties. He'd left behind an entire way of life to travel the world and have new adventures. He had found a job with the local government and spent his nights cooking strange meals and exploring the world with a vigor and genuineness that defied simple descriptions.

"Brandolon, tell me: what does it mean in English, 'seduction'?" he asked in a conspicuous but clear French accent. We were venturing through deepening snow to pick up food from Tesco before a blizzard set in.

"Hmm. Why do you ask?" I replied.

"I told my boss that she is very seductive."

I laughed. "You did what?"

"She has a way of talking that captures an audience. Does this not mean the same thing in English?" he asked.

"Not really. It generally indicates you might want to … have sex with her," I replied.

"Oh really? That's what it means? In French it means not just sex."

"Well, how did she respond?" I asked. I was not smooth, nor gifted with an alluring French accent. I also looked like a broke teenager with my unkempt and still-growing dreadlocks and limited wardrobe. I grew embarrassed just thinking of the response I'd have received.

"She smiled. Said we should get a drink sometime," he replied.

That's Charles.

The group of us shared a two-bedroom flat on the seventeenth floor of a tower in Camden Town, just up the hill from the Chalk Farm tube station.

It was late 2010. The recession was still stunting the world. I didn't know where I would end up next. But I grew into a kind of peace and happiness that belied my precarious financials. Messay and I talked for six to ten hours every day. We shared fears and passions. Every moment without her voice felt like an eternity. I grew to know the rest of my classmates better. There were Italian, German, French, Chinese, Canadian, and American students—voices and minds from all over the world.

Together, we visited the UN in Geneva. We drank pint after pint and glass after glass of wine as we met diplomats, ambassadors, famous economists, and other scholars. We talked with the head of the IMF, the chief mediators for the Sierra Leone conflict and conflicts between white South Africans and Nelson Mandela's African National Congress party, and the man who led the training of Eritrean diplomats after their independence from Ethiopia. I thrilled at this new direction my studies were taking me. Possibility and hope, those abandoned promises from Obama's campaign trail, began to awaken within me again. My dream of becoming a foreign service officer faded farther and farther into the past as I grew closer to what I had been inspired to pursue during my time as a radio producer.

I was no longer simply helping to relay amazing ideas. I was an active part of an entire world of ideas. And that world represented a new kind of freedom. Thinking back now, I know that I was deep within a process of reimagining my ambitions at their core. I was coming to understand my desires—those dreams of a better world balanced with that urge for

I was no Longer simply Helping To reLay amazing iDeas. I was an active Part OF an enTire WOrLD OF iDeas.

personal freedom—and then interrogating the many ways I might satisfy them beyond the limited scope of ambition in which I had invested so much faith and hope at an earlier time.

CHAPTER SEVENTEEN

SOMETHING'S NOT RIGHT

Messay was there to greet me when I touched down in Dallas. She had straightened her hair. Her caramel skin seemed to have lightened and changed over the winter months. We embraced, and there was one undeniable fact: she had only grown more beautiful in my eyes. I was deep in love and had truly longed to see her again after a year of long-distance calls and letters.

Dallas seemed foreign to me. More than ever before, I felt that its energies could not sustain me. The bland strip malls that dotted our drive from the airport into the city, the endless sun—what value were these qualities without their opposites, without clear points of tension and contrast?

As we approached the city center, my reaction was then as it had been before, and as it remains to this day. I found the shallow vanity of those glass skyscrapers and bridges to nowhere to be almost repugnant. None of these things were indications of humans thriving or even just living good-enough lives. I wanted better for myself, better for Messay, better for my mom and everyone I loved.

I had spent almost a year in London, often struggling to find the money for food or to take the bus to campus. I would walk miles from Camden Town to Russell Square just for classes. Nevertheless, while there, I'd never felt more certain of who I was and who I aspired to be. London had already become home, a place synonymous with free thinking over pints on the big topics of the day. I felt as though my gamble had paid off, and in the process, I'd begun to taste that new kind of freedom. Financial freedom may have continued to elude me, but I had experienced the freedom to think, to speak and be heard, to join in meaningful conversations, to feel that I'd moved beyond the limitations heaped on me by my circumstances and the many preconceptions and stereotypes held by others.

> FINANCIAL FREEDOM MAY HAVE CONTINUED TO ELUDE ME, BUT I HAD EXPERIENCED THE FREEDOM TO THINK, TO SPEAK AND BE HEARD, TO FEEL THAT I'D MOVED BEYOND THE LIMITATIONS HEAPED ON ME BY MY CIRCUMSTANCES.

After a couple of days back in town, I was able to spend time with my mother. While I'd been away in London, she had finally raised the funds to escape the apartment building of the slum-lord who, in the middle of a hot Texas summer, had refused to fix the broken AC or make any repairs. He had wanted everyone to leave the building so that he could sell the property. And he succeeded. Yet my mother's escape from that situation had not brought any more certainty.

"I want a place of my own. I want my own place," my mother said. We were driving down a highway that intersects the city. To the south, low-rise single-family homes. To the north, the glories of the Dallas skyline and the products of all the city's wealth.

"Okay, I can try to help you get a place." For reasons I didn't fully understand, she'd grown weary and agitated with her boyfriend Edward. He'd been in my mother's life for quite a while, and I'd begun to grow close to him since first returning to Dallas after undergrad in Pennsylvania. While I was focused on grad school, she had found a place with him in the Dallas suburb of Garland after leaving her own apartment. But she'd since left and was at this point migrating from place to place, staying with friends or her sisters. I couldn't mention his name to her now without instantly igniting her anger. I was happy to try to help her have a place of her own. The only question was how. Just back from grad school, I was still unemployed.

"You know, I'm still looking for a job. So I don't have much right now. How much do you make?"

"I make about $1,500 a month," she replied as we glided toward East Dallas and lunch.

Barbecue. I'd missed brisket about as much as I had Messay. I'd never tell her that, of course.

It had grown noticeably difficult to speak with my mother. She seemed alternatingly lost in a haze or almost intentionally dense, as if she were purposely trying to get a rise out of me.

"Is that enough to get your own place and have this car? You're still paying on it, right?" I asked.

"Yeah, it's enough," she replied, agitated. "You can help me too. Any little bit would help."

She was right about the last part. I wanted to help. But I had serious questions about the possibility of her getting her own place. As we added up the numbers, there was simply no way she could have her own apartment (even at the low end of the average rent price), keep the car (which she needed for work), and pay all her other bills and obligations.

"You think I'm like a child!" she yelled at me as I rounded out the numbers. I was shocked into silence. She was normally so calm and composed. "I'm not your child. I raised you!" And then: "I don't need you to believe I can do anything. You're just like everyone else."

"I'm just saying the damn numbers don't add up."

As I always say, I like to believe that I'm calm and rational, but I am also fully aware that no one is as adept at shattering that illusion as a parent. I, too, became enraged. We screamed at one another. She refused to accept my numbers, although her own math was so clearly in error.

I wanted nothing more than to help her. No one knew how much I owed her more than me. We had talked regularly during my time in London. I was aware that she had continued to struggle, yet every month without fail she had sent me one hundred dollars. That money had been a lifeline, often helping me to eat for weeks, even though I knew that she could barely afford it. Yet she had insisted on sending it, and I wrote her grateful letters in response.

From: Gwen Smith
To: me
Wednesday, January 5, 2011, 3:22 PM

Happy New Year, Brandolon!

I don't mean to be partial, but how is my favorite son? I got your message, but I lost my phone again. I will have to buy another one. I guess I will have to glue this one to my buttocks.

Anyway, say hello to Messay for me. I hope you had a great holiday together.

Love,
Mom

Oh, by the way, check your account. Didn't have much.

From: Brandolon Barnett
To: Gwen Smith
Thursday, January 13, 2011, 9:22 PM

If you could send anything in the next 24 hours or so I would really appreciate it? Either way, you've been a great mom to me and I really appreciate your help. This is the home stretch and though I can't say for sure given my luck, I think this is the last time I'll be needing any help. Messay helped me out a bit and my tax return will be good, but in the meantime my second check from the school is taking forever ... I've started my second term. My classes this term are

- International Economics
- Power in World Politics
- General Diplomatic Studies and Practice
- And Mandarin Chinese Language

I've started applying for jobs in Dallas (and London?) as well. Will is coming to visit me on the 23rd. I wish you could come as well but I know it can be hard. I hope this finds you well. I try to call you all the time but you never answer ... Anyway, have a good day mummy. Love ya. PS I know you probably won't be very interested but I've attached a couple of my papers if you're interested in reading them or can see the ... screen ...

Love ya mummy,
Brandolon

I knew all this, and I wanted to help. But I couldn't. Not yet. I literally had nothing. Without Messay to help me settle back in, I would have been as destitute as I'd feared back on the streets in northern Thailand.

We sat in silence over our barbecue, interjecting the odd inappropriate joke. That was our thing. I remembered back to when I'd given her a key to my first apartment. One Friday, I'd come home early from work. It was a beautiful day. Bottle of wine in hand, I was planning to watch the latest episode of *Fringe* (a superior version of the *X-Files*) and head out on the town. I was committed to having some fun. I had just been paid, and it was one of those months when paydays fell such that I got three checks instead of just two.

I walked into the apartment to find my mother on my couch. She'd just cleaned the entire apartment for me. I was agitated but thanked her begrudgingly. Then I approached her on the couch, took that paycheck cash (all the cash I had in the world) out of my pocket, and gently slapped her face with it. "Have you ever been slapped in the face with a thousand dollars?" I asked. She gasped; at first, she was irate, and then she started laughing as she swore she'd get me back. The very next day, as I sat on the couch hungover and still finishing that same episode of *Fringe*, she came into my apartment and slapped me in the face with *two* thousand dollars she'd taken out of her own paycheck and savings just for the occasion. We laughed.

These were the memories I had of her—our teasing humor, our good conversations, always her smile and support, and her high energy.

I looked across the table at her, tensions from our argument subsiding. This was the first time I really saw her since coming home from London. She had always looked young for her age—at forty-five she could easily have passed for thirty-five, at fifty for forty. When I'd left in the fall of 2010, we had hugged and cried. I knew that she would miss me, but I could see the pride in her eyes and that smile behind her tears. Now, sitting across from her just over a year later, I could barely believe what I saw. She had lost so much weight, she was emaciated. There was a look in her eyes that lingered between smiles and bouts of fiery anger; her light seemed noticeably dimmed.

How well do we understand why we do the things we do? How well do we know why we dream what we dream? I think that so much of the energy that animates us and moves us forward comes from unknown sources and so much of our motivation from unacknowledged reasons.

Here I was feeling triumphant after completing the first half of my graduate program. I had a renewed sense of purpose from my studies and travels and felt I'd gotten back on track. But until I was sitting there across from my mother, I had not fully realized how much of what I'd done was for her.

And the last thing I'd imagined was how completely I could question what all my effort was really worth. During my time away, she had clearly become ill. Something was wrong.

I continued to watch her, wondering to myself what might have happened. Sad and in disbelief, I hoped that I was mistaken.

CHAPTER EIGHTEEN

survival

I drove my mother from doctor's office to doctor's office. I was twenty-five years old, fresh out of my stint in London. All that remained was to complete my master's thesis. After seeing how much her health had deteriorated, I resolved to stay in Dallas and complete my degree remotely rather than return to London. I had no job. I had no idea what I was doing. And I was responsible for taking care of my mother when I could still barely take care of myself.

The US healthcare system had us running in loops. My mother's meager healthcare coverage would pay for only enough care to treat a symptom. Then, ignored, other symptoms would emerge only to be halfheartedly treated once again. The blood vessels in her eyes would burst while she waited for a bus. I would go to pick her up to take her to the eye doctor. We would nearly go bankrupt treating it. And then it would repeat. Her legs would swell, then return to normal after she'd be given some expensive medication. Then, the swelling would return.

With each doctor visit, I pieced together the story of the past year.

While I had been in London, her faculties had deteriorated. I didn't know why, but it was clear that she was not understanding what the doctors were telling her. It was also clear that they didn't care enough to notice. As we were being rushed in and out of waiting rooms and exam rooms, it dawned on me with increasing clarity—particularly given my own recent revelations about the reasons behind my own ambitions—that no one was asking why. *Why* was she struggling with all these symptoms? What were the underlying reasons for her ailments?

Each day took a little bit more from her. She stayed with relatives. My oldest aunt cared deeply, but the same condition that kept my mother from fully grasping the doctor's recommendations also kept my mother from seeing her sister's affections. They fought. Though I was fresh from learning about mediation from some of the world's greatest minds, I was utterly powerless to help negotiate their relationship.

So my mother bounced from home to home, still absolutely unwilling to stay with Edward, her boyfriend of nine years. I searched for jobs, desperate to find something, anything, that would quickly let me do more to help her.

Messay and I found an apartment. I finally found a part-time job as a contractor with a local foundation. I would be making $30,000 a year to run an environmental magazine as part of one of their initiatives. Dallas was not exactly the place to be for using my international studies degree or international economics expertise. I had taken a risk to travel halfway around the world, accrued tens of thousands of dollars in debt, and come home once again to that same sense of despair and helplessness.

I understood that my career prospects would be better served in a place like DC, where there were many jobs that could help me do work that matched the core of my ambitions. But how could I leave my mother alone after all that she had done for me? I knew more and more with each passing day that so much of what I had done—the risks, the travels—was for her. I wanted to make her proud of me. And I wanted to help her find a better place in this world. I wanted *her* world to be better.

During these months, I daydreamed of her getting better. I would take a job in DC doing good work and making good money. I would save and buy her a little bar with a piano in the corner. She could sing to patrons on the weekends, make new friends, and have her own adventures. I wanted her to come to London in seven months, after I'd completed my thesis, to see my graduation. It would be the first time she'd left the country, but definitely not the last. She would get to hear that choir in South Africa, see the temples of Japan and Thailand, feel the mad energy of Shanghai, and taste the foods of Brazil and Venezuela.

I took on a new mission—to find whatever ladder I could to climb from the job I had found and to break past the salary ceiling that had seemingly been slammed shut over my head. All I wanted was to make more than $50K. With that, Messay and I could continue to have our own place, but in a place like Dallas where costs are low, I could also help my mother get an apartment of her own. She'd continued to beg for that freedom, and I wanted that for her even though I questioned whether she was capable of taking care of herself any longer.

The foundation where I worked was established by a wealthy heiress. While I recognized her good intentions, I questioned how the organization was structured, along with its priorities. My experience of crowdfunding and citizen philanthropy had changed the course of my life when I'd raised funds for grad school, but this first brush with private family philanthropy opened my eyes to the extent to which philanthropic dollars can be tossed into an endless void.

My immediate supervisor, the executive director of the foundation, brought empathy and understanding to his work. So did his assistant. Together, they seemed to me to have an interest in guiding the organization toward a clearer strategy and greater impact. But their goals were also entangled with the wishes of the founder. It was an interesting dynamic to observe, especially during an ongoing global recession. The world had made the value of every single dollar so clear. To not spend wisely when surrounded by such despair and need seemed even more of a waste of a precious resource.

THE WORLD HAD MADE THE VALUE OF EVERY SINGLE DOLLAR SO CLEAR. TO NOT SPEND WISELY WHEN SURROUNDED BY SUCH DESPAIR AND NEED SEEMED EVEN MORE OF A WASTE OF A PRECIOUS RESOURCE.

Soon enough, it was 2011, and the financial crisis seemed to be waning. I still couldn't find a decent full-time job with benefits, but it seemed the worst of the recession might be behind us as a nation. And attention was shifting from the recession to other matters. The Tea Party was gathering strength on the right, the Occupy Wall Street movement on the left. I attended Occupy meetings, because the work I was doing was making me feel that we were at the point at which inequality was inescapably visible—a genuine reality of American society. My mother's struggle to survive after a lifetime of hard work was part of that story. I also watched other stories unfold, stories of the immense wealth and privilege that shielded a small few from the world the rest of us had grown to know the hard way.

In addition to the magazine, I started a regional environmental awards program—the Dallas Fort Worth (DFW) Sustainable Leadership Awards. I oversaw triple digit increases in the site's readership and views. I got involved in the organization's international efforts, helping Māori researchers with a project at the Menil Collection in Houston to recover lost artifacts. I was completing my master's thesis on the interplay between local cultural industries and economic development, so that work in particular was interesting to me.

In short, and as I'd always done, I infused my everyday work with my passions, finding little pieces of the man I wanted to be and the work I wanted to do in the world. Nevertheless, I was just a freelancer at the foundation, a 1099 employee. This was not the stability I'd glimpsed in the days after passing the Foreign Service exam. It felt like another kind of limbo.

My mother's condition worsened as the months went on. Doctor and hospital visits transformed to longer hospital stays.

"Hey mamma jamma," I called to her gently one day. The hospital room was beige. I was sitting in a chair in the corner of the room. A hospital official had just come in to work with us so that I could have power of attorney over her affairs. She was struggling to breathe, her legs swollen to the size of small trees. Fluid dripped from them. Her eyes were bloody, and her lovely short hair tangled. She lay there in her robes as I spoke.

"Yes dear," she responded through beleaguered breaths. The tubes in her nose rose and fell with such harsh deliberation. She was fighting. I wanted her to know I was fighting too.

"I got a raise. They made me full time at the foundation. I'm gonna be making over fifty thousand dollars. So I can help you more." Thinking back on it now, I feel so selfish. I wanted her to feel some sense of security, to know that together we could get her back on her feet. But I also just wanted her to be proud of me again and to see that I was trying to be the person she hoped I might be one day.

"That's so lovely, dear. You should take Messay out for a nice dinner." She spoke quietly. I remember a ray of sunlight peeking through the half-opened blinds. Her eyes were on the ceiling. Her focus so clearly on each labored breath. I don't know that she really heard me.

"I told your mother she was dying three years ago, Mr. Barnett. I'm so sorry."

It was a day later. I had finally found the "coordinating physician." This was the answer to my question about what tied all my mother's symptoms together. The coordinating physician was beautiful: tall, brown skin, and long, dark hair. Her beauty felt out of place as I stared at her, there in her white coat, stating horrors so matter-of-factly.

"I don't understand." I finally squeezed out a reply. "What's wrong with her?"

"There're complications from lupus, I'm afraid," was her reply.

Lupus? My mother had told me years ago that she'd been diagnosed, but she'd also told me it was in check. I even felt sure I could remember her saying it had gone into remission. I fell back into the cold chair, head in my hands.

"I'm so sorry to have to tell you this." She touched my shoulder, and then she was gone. I walked to the waiting area. Messay was there. I fell into her arms in disbelief. I told the rest of the family. The wondering and worrying had consumed us all for months. I refused to accept the truth.

That night she was discharged from her long hospital stay to hospice, which would be set up in an apartment I'd gotten for her. After a long wait, I was finally able to help. But now there would be another kind of wait.

I believed that I could fix things. I had seen so much, survived so many little disasters. I'd traveled the world chasing a dream, always with the yawning jaws of abject poverty threatening to swallow me whole. Taken together, were these moments not miracles? Were they not proof that I could overcome whatever obstacle? That anything could be fixed with enough resources and ingenuity? I would save her. I had some resources now, with my raise and promotion.

"You've gotten so fat," she said. She was feeling energetic and talkative. It was a beautiful Sunday morning.

I laughed. "I've eaten a lot of pizzas over the last few years. But things are getting better. I'll lose it."

I held her hand as the sun rose to its zenith. She asked about work. About Messay. I told her I was in love. She said she knew it. Told me I was lucky. To take good care of Messay. She told me I'd found good people. She wished she could have helped me more but was glad that they were all there for me, able to help me go to school and get good grades. She told me to take care of Will, my adopted brother from college, who by this point she'd met on many occasions. She even called him her other son. We were both only children of single mothers. She was glad that we had found family in each other.

I told my mother stories about London—describing Buckingham Palace and the Thames, my adventures on the tube and the night bus, in pubs and clubs. I told her how I'd finally learned there was a place that could feel like home to me. She told me I got that wanderlust from her—she'd always dreamed of traveling. She also warned me not to drink too much, like my dad. As a child, I'd met him once or twice when he took me to McDonald's and got me some shoes from Family Dollar. I told her that I was happy to be earning more, that I wanted to make the world better but also wanted to feel free, free to not worry about money every day. She understood. She was proud of me.

Somewhere in the time between afternoon and evening, my aunt knocked on the door. Messay had been waiting in the other room all these hours while my mother and I spoke. Messay and I were both tired and hungry. I agreed to get some food. I let go of my mother's hand and said goodbye. She was watched over. She was loved. Messay and I walked a few blocks down empty Dallas streets to an IHOP. Messay held my hand and made me laugh and smile.

Family members had gathered in the apartment as we returned. When next I stood beside my mother's bed, she was gone from this world.

CHAPTER NINETEEN

WHEN THEY'RE GONE

To me, it's not so much the time you miss with a parent when they're gone. It's the knowledge of their presence. In every moment up until that last, until the end, my mother was there with me. I could be on safari in Tanzania, seeing a moon bigger than any moon I'd ever seen, listening to unknown primates playing among the treetops, hearing hippos bellow in a distant valley. But the knowledge persisted, deep in my mind, that if I could just get to a phone or write up an email, she'd be there. *She'll be there.* I'd always felt that she would be, and she always was.

Until the end.

There is a story of that end. My mother, with her greatest secret painfully laid bare, lay there with tubes growing from her like cruelly winding vines. Her labored breaths told that great hidden truth over and over. Each rise and fall of her chest told the secret that she'd known all along: she was dying.

She hid it. For years.

By not telling, she kept me from saving her. She left me alone with regret and with the image of her laid to waste, defeated by finances, by gravity, and by her own body, her dignity trampled. I can't but see her there, unable to move, unable to think, unable to speak. Each breath an endless despair and a crippling shame. Her secret robbed me of everything, but what still hurts most was the loss of opportunities to make her proud, to remind her that all I did was for her, to achieve the life she'd always asked me to strive for.

The self-questioning and self-doubt grew incessant: Why didn't I make more money sooner so I could take care of her earlier? Why didn't I realize what was happening? Why didn't I go to all the doctors' appointments from the start? Why had I been so selfish as to think that my passions mattered? Why was I off in London, drinking and loving, touring and playing, learning and dreaming, while the person in the world who knew me best, held me the longest, withered to nothingness? How could I have failed as I tried so hard to succeed?

The questions pulled against my soul, pushed down on my heart, and robbed me of my breath. They also fueled my rage.

That story, which consumed me for years after her passing, held no truth. At least no truth but my own vanity.

There is another story of that end.

What *if* she had told me?

I would have given up my dreams to fight a fight that doctors told her could not be won. Those breaths did not lay bare some shameful truth. Instead, each labored heave was a testament to her courage and strength to go it alone for my sake. Her dignity was not trampled. She suffered with pride and stubbornness. All for me. She kept a secret, hid her pain, went to surgery and let herself be cut without telling me. All to protect the dreams she had for so long fostered within me. That yearning within me to see a world bigger than any world she and I would ever have known, that strength to survive tragedy and disastrous happenstance—it's all from her.

I have experienced so much of the world because of my mother's courage and because of the small piece of it that I inherited. I have met different people and participated in traditions from tea ceremonies in Kyoto to Candomblé in Brazil. I've seen elephants in the streets of Bangkok, temples among the throngs in Tokyo, mists among the mountains of China, palaces among the ruins of Laos, beaches along the coasts of Costa Rica.

Yet I have never seen, and may never see again, that courage, the indomitable desire to help and protect someone you love. One could see all the world and never encounter that presence that was my mother. It is her presence that I miss.

But even though faded from a tangible reality, my mother's presence has transformed into hope, into inspiration. Her courage makes me wish that I, too, one day, will follow in her footsteps and protect the dreams of those I love at all cost.

CHAPTER TWENTY

Artist and Creation

Months went by. Everything was fine. That's what I told myself. That's what I told Messay and everyone around me.

Everything wasn't fine. With my mother gone, I felt aimless. I focused on the realization that so much of my motivation came from my desire to be seen as someone worthy of her sacrifices. I felt sure that I was not. I couldn't even tell whether she really and truly knew how much I cared for her and admired her strength. I still struggle to forgive myself for not being there the moment she left the world behind. I'm told she called my name. I was at an IHOP eating some mediocre chicken tenders.

So much of my journey has been about questioning the pre-conceptions and stereotypes in my own head and trying to move beyond them. If I could go back in time, now, I would ask my younger self: Why do you want the career you want? That job, that title? Why do you want the money you want? If anything, asking and honestly answering these questions has helped me plot a path past those dark times, the ones that eventually come for us all. Coming to the truth of the "why" behind my career and financial aspirations has allowed me to understand that there were many paths toward the things I held dear, not just the one or two with the heft and respect that comes from a particular title and a long-standing social perception.

SO MUCH OF MY JOURNEY HAS BEEN ABOUT QUESTIONING THE PRECONCEPTIONS AND STEREOTYPES IN MY OWN HEAD AND TRYING TO MOVE BEYOND THEM.

I'd held on to that deep, visceral desire to have and to know true freedom, and more and more I understood that could only come from making my own unencumbered choices. Another of my strongest desires was to be there for my mother. Unfortunately, that realization had come uneasily and too late. And weren't these desires at odds with one another? I wanted to be unencumbered, to have the freedom to choose my own fate, but I also wanted to acknowledge the constraints on my choices, to make, for my mother, a sacrifice like the one she had made for me.

After she died, I continued to struggle financially. As a contractor, I had foregone paying self-employment taxes during the time my mother was ill. Instead, I'd used the money to help her with doctors' visits and to make sure she could keep her phone, pay her bills, have food, and in those last weeks, have the home of her own that she'd longed for.

Her life insurance had left me a little money—about $20K—more than I had ever had at one time. Well over half of it went toward the funeral costs.

The remaining funds? I didn't want them. Looking at my bank statements made me physically ill. For my mother's death to have been the event that finally gave me enough financial space to breathe, that I had found some freedom in her death, was more than I could bear. For the moment, I was no longer on the knife's edge, but I could hardly find a reason to get out of bed.

I was told that she would have wanted me to go on living. So I did. I looked for new opportunities in an economy that had theoretically emerged from its worst downturn in eighty years. My search started by looking at jobs that seemed perfect matches for my experience and qualifications. These were primarily in DC and New York, where large multilateral institutions, development agencies, and philanthropic organizations were typically based. My desire to do some good in the world—to leave it a better place than I'd found it and pay back the love and kindness which had been shown to me—was dimmed but not extinguished.

I applied for program officer roles at more rigorous foundations and program associate roles at large USAID contractors. Forty applications in, I had no responses.

I then considered jobs within these organizations using skills unrelated to my master's degree but connected to my undergraduate degree: communications, media production, writing and content creation, program coordination.

It was around this point that I decided to keep track of my activities in a spreadsheet. Seventy resumes submitted and still no responses.

Messay was thriving. She had taken to heart the advice I'd given from my own experiences to connect whenever possible her passions with her work and practical skills. This was the idea of achieving, little by little, a life where a larger and larger percentage of time and energy can be devoted to the things that help you feel energized and motivated every day to be your very best and to overcome any risks or obstacles. She ran with it in ways that I could only imagine and was thriving in a job using her accounting skills to get closer to her passion for the arts. She'd become the staff accountant for the Dallas Black Dance Theatre, one of the premier Black dance companies in the world.

We had moved into a junior one-bedroom in the Oak Lawn neighborhood of Dallas. Both of us had an idea to build our bed out of my old *Encyclopaedia Britannica*s. We made a cozy home.

I don't know if Messay knew it, but her success and joy, the many complimentary performances I joined her at, and the moments we were able to spend exploring new restaurants, new galleries, new bars, and other spaces, is all that sustained me. I'm convinced it kept me alive, if not literally then certainly figuratively. I felt I had to make her proud as well.

Months went by. There were still times when I would think back to the Foreign Service exam, to what might have been. Still working from home for the foundation but feeling more and more marginalized and useless in my role, I would sit for hours on our couch and stare into space. The morning sun would often turn to dusk, and I would not have eaten and would have barely moved.

I just needed a way into something better. I needed someone to see my resume, read my cover letter, believe that I could do something, and just call me back. I was one hundred applications in and still no responses.

I changed tactics again. I used my middle name to sound less "ethnic." I decided I would take a role as an executive assistant within any of these organizations—anything just to get in the door and show what I was capable of, how quickly I could learn and adapt. Almost two hundred resumes in; no responses.

My adopted brother Will, Messay, her sister, and I all ventured to London for my graduation. I saw old faces, remembered the struggle and the thrill. But every corner I turned, every congratulations, every photo taken was a reminder that my mother was missing. To this day, I don't have any photos of my graduation. It was a bittersweet trip.

Messay was applying to grad schools in arts management programs. She wanted to run a symphony one day. Even on the heels of graduating from my degree program, some part of me felt bitter as she thrived and embarked on an adventure that I felt was still only half complete for me. I sensed that my own adventure might never lead me *anywhere*. I was being left behind.

It was a reaction for which I felt and still feel such shame.

Well over two hundred resumes in, I succumbed. I had to do anything, find anything, to support myself. I needed a job that paid more, a job that had benefits and that gave me some relief from constant financial worry. I needed to be more than a contractor wrangling self-employment taxes with no job security and no ability to help the person I loved. I applied to anything and everything.

I started thinking about how the only opportunities for me resided in cities that I could not afford to live in. Too many people struggle in this way, their potential untapped due only to their physical location in a world where we regularly meet and work with colleagues across continents.

It was almost a year after my mother's passing that we got the news: Messay had gotten a full scholarship to Carnegie Mellon in Pittsburgh to attain a master's in arts management. I threw her a surprise party to celebrate. I told her I would take care of arrangements with the apartment. Just leave it to me. And then we counted down the months.

The drive from Dallas to Pittsburgh was lovely. We stopped in Memphis and Nashville along the way. Barbecue and blues on Beale Street. Country music and shots of Fireball in downtown Nashville. Hours in the car, driving and dreaming of her future. Her energy and excitement were infectious. It was the closest we had ever been. I helped her settle in and enjoyed a few days in Pittsburgh.

Messay and I in Memphis

Despite my mother's heartfelt and earnest attempts to make it so, I'm not a religious man. I have for a long time held a belief in what I call the essential nature of creation. I always imagine an artist in a gallery. They stand smiling, proud, surrounded by their greatest works and achievements. Each canvas tells a story of all they hold dear, connections to their deepest memories and most vulnerable moments.

The doors swing open. In comes the first group of explorers. The artist watches them closely, filled with anticipation. Will they like these works? Will my art inspire them? Will it change them? Enlighten them? Will it spur them to new love or give rise to thoughts that I myself might never have imagined?

Then the artist notices something strange. The explorers are not engaging fully with his creations. Instead, one by one, they bow at his feet. To me, this isn't the reaction any creator would seek.

I don't know if this way of thinking about creation or my love for Keats came first. Regardless, that image of the artist standing in anticipation of others enjoying his or her creations, that's what formed the core of what you might call my "religion." It was a thought that, God or no god, our duty to *any* creator was to engage with their creation. To take inspiration from it, to explore it as fully as we can. Worship, within this framework, is of little to no value.

Warm, midday sun shone through the windows of her new apartment. Outside, fall was setting in. The seasons were changing. But what about me? I felt that any hope I had for a career—and the freedom, meaning, and good story that I'd anticipated would come with it—all that was fading. Now, in my last days with Messay before she embarked on her new adventure, my bitterness was also growing. It was 2013, my mother was gone, Messay was going off to pursue her dream, and I was alone. For someone who had set out to fly, I felt that I'd not moved an inch in six years.

Messay was getting ready to enjoy our last day together before I headed back to an empty apartment. I felt I had no more answers. No more hope. I was stripped bare. There was nothing else I could do that I had not done.

What I'm about to recount I do not share lightly. I believe in science, in research, and in data. Yet in that moment, I got down on my knees. I thought to myself, *What if sometimes we cannot interpret the world, cannot make sense of the creation. In those times, is it okay to look to the artist for guidance?* I asked my mother to help me. I prayed to a Christian God to whom I had not spoken nor even thought about since I was a child. "Help me," I said. "I can't do this anymore. I can't do this on my own."

Ten minutes later, I got a call from an international NGO based in San Francisco. In my desperation, I'd applied for a "returnship" there—an unpaid internship for midcareer professionals, recent graduate students with some professional experience, and others attempting to reset their careers. I'd applied to be an "NGO and corporate services" intern, which meant that I would help evaluate NGOs and nonprofits for potential partnerships with US companies. I would also assist with work that helped companies craft corporate social responsibility strategies by providing support to a corporate services team in the form of research and reports.

We spoke for a few minutes. The woman on the other end seemed nice. I think now, when I make job offers, about whether I'm changing someone's life. I'm utterly sure she had no idea she was changing mine. The work was unpaid and most definitely not glamorous. I wasn't excited. In fact, I felt instead the sting of failure. But I thought back to that moment only minutes before. I had not become religious. But I did feel … watched over? And I felt like I knew one thing clearly.

This opportunity was mine. I had to take it.

After bittersweet goodbyes, I caught a flight back to Dallas. I unlocked the door to our apartment and broke down in tears. I felt alone. Truly alone. But I had a next destination, a new mission.

I used part of what my mother had left me to get a car, a small used convertible from Pontiac, another one of those castoffs from our Great Recession.

I felt it was important to use part of what she left me on something I could love. I had only what remained of the money my mother had left me and the small monthly one-hundred-dollar pension payment I would get every month for the rest of my life—the same amount she had given me in grad school. Good friends had given me money to support my move—more philanthropy. I'd also planned to stay with my adopted brother, Will, and his mother to cut costs.

I managed to pawn and donate a few things, but with only days to prepare and get from Dallas to San Francisco, Messay and I agreed to just throw away many of the things we had acquired for our apartment. I loaded up my little two-door car with every possession I had in the world and fired up my phone's GPS.

Dallas, Texas, to San Francisco, California, is twenty-seven hours by way of Albuquerque and Flagstaff, Arizona.

The money I had wasn't enough to hold out for long. I had a time limit for finding work that paid, another new path. In other words, I was adding another gamble to my growing list. But the clock was ticking. It was time to drive.

CHAPTER TWENTY-ONE

THE Drive

Just as my ambitions evolved over time as I better understood the core reasons for my desires, my understanding of the many kinds of freedom we can find and enjoy in this world has evolved too. It was on this trip, for example, that I acknowledged that yes, there is the financial freedom that I was still seeking, but there is also the kind of freedom that the open road offers. I might not be a fan of Jack Kerouac, but I honestly couldn't deny that feeling of independence I had throughout the drive. I may have still been racked with guilt over my mother's passing and my shame at my jealousy of the woman I loved and the path she was on. I may have been filled with constant worry and concern over how I would eat, pay my bills, and pay my debts. I may have still felt like a failure, as all my attempts just to find good work had been met with not so much as a single interview invitation. Yet amid all this, the landscapes of midwestern America were soothing medicine.

It was late summer 2013. My future was on the clock, and my ambition had sent me west like some nineteenth-century prospector searching for a better life amid the gold rush. Still, there on the open road, I was finally alone with my grief, my bitter disappointment in myself and my perceived failures, and even my anger. Over three days, a full range of emotions I'd tried to bury revealed themselves to me.

Driving through the plains of Texas, endless green space unfolds before you, from the tip of your nose to as far as the eye can see, interrupted only by massive windmills looming on the horizon. Driving past smaller and smaller towns, I better understood the typical southern and conservative mindset than I could have without ever having seen these wide-open spaces. The horizon stretched on endlessly such that anything anyone built or created, any change they made to the natural landscape, could be viewed for miles in any direction. That alone, I imagined, could make one feel huge, powerful, and completely disconnected from the rest of the world. In other words, it could be very easy to live here and tell yourself that all you had to do to be successful was to go out there, claim a piece of land, and put in the hard work to make it all yours.

The plains of Texas

The only places I'd been to in Texas were Dallas, Austin, Houston, San Antonio, and Fort Worth—all large American cities. Things there were different. Every street, every corner, every bus stop or train station made it easy to see the interconnectedness of people and place, the inevitable impact your neighbor's actions had on your life and the lives of those you loved. It was easy to feel small as one among millions or to picture your freedom as dependent on rising, and ranking, above them.

To the contrary, this wide-open empty space offered a different kind of freedom than the other kind I had grasped at, one born from the sheer enormity of open spaces and low population density. It made me wonder even more about the systems of competition we've put in place, the definitions of "success" we chase after, and how those things can imprison us.

I'd been nearly destitute in Dallas, but could I have bought my mother land out here? Could we have made something different of our lives in this place? And now, here I was driving along, asking myself: Do I have the strength left to seize my own piece of the world?

The signal from the North Texas NPR affiliate and its familiar voices, the voices of friends and former colleagues, faded as the miles flew by. Another comfort lost. Empty truck stops with rattlesnake warnings were my only company. Hoping to save, Cheetos were my only nourishment.

DO I HAVE THE STRENGTH LEFT TO SEIZE MY OWN PIECE OF THE WORLD?

Texas lasted from dawn to dusk. No sooner had I settled into the plains than they began a slow transformation to desert. As the dusk turned to evening, shadows rose in the distance. Small hills and what seemed a splash of new colors were visible in the fading light. Those shadowy hills, cast in relief against the dim moonlight and bright lights of cities that I would pass, were like ghosts that multiplied as I drove deep into the night. Twelve hours into my drive, I stopped in the parking lot of a national park, pushed my seat back the few inches it could go, and stared out at a world I had never seen. In all my travels, these scenes from the American roadside were as unique in their beauty as anything I'd yet come across. My yearning for adventure was being satiated. For the first time in months, for the first time since my mother had passed, I fell asleep thrilled again to think of tomorrow.

The next day brought more desert. The colors that had only been hinted at in the previous day's few dusky minutes and many moonlit hours now sprang to life with the sun. As I approached Arizona, I felt surrounded by colors from a John Wayne western—every shade of orange and tan. It was late summer. I rolled down the windows to feel the blasts of intense heat. The thought of walking even an inch into that endless expanse of sand and rock was enough to make me shiver and push the pedal to the floor. With the luck I'd been having, I could just see the car breaking down in the middle of the desert on the New Mexico-Arizona border.

I'd never been further west than Texas. As I drove, this whole new world opened up to me and swallowed my sorrows. I pride myself on always grounding my thoughts in broader contexts, so as that new world flew by, I could not help but think of all the people that had come this way before. On foot. On horseback. By wagon. With no AC! No NPR or podcasts! No Metric, no Red Hot Chili Peppers, no Phantogram or Florence and the Machine. All they had was this beauty to push and console them, this heat and this endless expanse that was at once both welcoming and terrifying.

The thought of those that came before—of *their* struggles, *their* wild gambles, *their* rides out into the unknown—to say that feeling of connection to the past reinvigorated me would be an understatement. I didn't know what the future would bring, but I know now that this long and lonesome trip began a process of healing for me in which I slowly felt less alone. My journey had taken on the feeling of pilgrimage, and slowly but surely, hope began to break through my despair. I hoped that this might be some essential part of my story, that I could still win out against time and the looming fear of abject failure. There was still so much to see! How could I just give up? My mother hadn't held on to her secret and died in pain so that I could just... stop trying.

I have said many times since that trip that there's power in knowing and even in imagining the struggles of others—power to heal and to push us forward. I hope that my story will empower others, lift someone as I was lifted by thoughts of the struggles of those who walked and rode those paths through the desert long before me and by memories of those whose actual struggles I had witnessed.

With each mile, I gained a sense of awe and wonder. From random truck stops framed by bright red earth and towering rock to the petrified forest, I felt at times like I had ventured to another planet.

Scenes from my drive west

I stopped and spent a day in Flagstaff. Hills had transformed to mountains that towered in the distance. Bright desert touched on lush green. I was approaching California.

I drove up and up into the mountains in the dawn light, then down again on winding roads cut with the force of human ingenuity. I was grateful for the cleared path.

After almost four days, I arrived in Santa Clara with my every possession in the world stuffed into that two-door coupe convertible. The South Bay—my home for now. I would be living in one of the most expensive places on the planet, commuting into the city to work for no pay. It couldn't last long. Time was still ticking, but I felt a new energy. My mother had sacrificed everything so that I could see and marvel at this world and all creation. That dark voice inside of me screamed, but I knew I couldn't give up.

CHAPTER TWENTY-TWO

MY Opportunity

My reward at the end of the road? A futon and an internship fueled by burritos. Taco Bell was a bit pricey, and the tacos from Jack in the Box were no bueno. So my everyday meal consisted of burritos from 7-Eleven and the occasional Totino's pepperoni pizza.

I was grateful. Will had taken me in when he himself was still struggling, like so many, with the fallout of the recession. There were three of us in a one-bedroom apartment in Santa Clara. Will and I shared the living room, and his mother, who had moved to California to be with him, was in the bedroom.

The international nonprofit for which I would be working was based in an incubator called the Impact Hub. Located in downtown

San Francisco on Mission and Fifth, the organization had a familiar mission. They built an online marketplace of international volunteering and giving opportunities. They also paired volunteers and companies with these initiatives. It was actually one of the jobs I'd applied to out of interest in getting exposure to the corporate social good/corporate social responsibility (CSR) movement. I'd be learning about various CSR programs and strategies in addition to vetting potential partners for them based on resources and priorities. After sending out hundreds of applications, I'd grown cynical about more traditional international development and philanthropic institutions; they didn't seem to want me or, from what I could tell, people like me (there were certainly scant few Black men among their ranks). From my own experiences and from witnessing my mother's struggle just to live

> I HaD aLSO grOWN TO BeLieve THaT PrOviDing SOmeOne WiTH STeaDy, WeLL-PaiD WOrk miGHT JUST DO mOre TO make THe WOrLD a BeTTer PLace THan a miLLiOn nOnPrOfiT iniTiaTives.

a life of dignity, I had also grown to believe that providing someone with steady, well-paid work might just do more to make the world a better place than a million nonprofit initiatives. I still had the same mission and the same drive, but my definition of what it meant to do good in the world was slowly but inexorably expanding, all because I had begun to ask myself "*why.*"

During the first days of my "returnship," I drove into the city, thinking that would be the most convenient mode of travel. These drives were my few daily moments of luxury. California in early fall was beautiful, so I would put the top down and ride into the city, past mountains and towns with anatopistic Spanish names: Santa Clara, San Jose, Palo Alto, San Bruno, San Mateo, names that eventually switched over to more familiar-sounding towns: Mountain View, Burlingame, Millbrae. Then there was nearby Sunnyvale. As a big fan of *Buffy the Vampire Slayer* and the fictional goings on in Sunny*dale*, that particular town's name always made me smile. What I wouldn't give to live in a fictional world right now, I thought, even one with vampires, slayers, demons, and witches struggling for supremacy over a mouth to hell.

Each morning the fog would roll in just as I approached the city, towers rising in the distance. Parking was thirty-five dollars. Needless to say, this little luxury didn't last long before I was making my way to work on the Caltrain.

I worked only two days a week, and it was fruitful. I sat on calls with major companies like Google and Cisco, taking notes as their foundation and CSR leaders described their philanthropic programs and strategies. In grad school, I had studied initiatives like the United Nations Global Compact, but this was a whole new world.

Compared to the work I'd engaged in before, here was an entirely different way of thinking about impact. Traditional philanthropy and the nonprofits and NGOs I'd yearned to be a part of sought to change the world through benevolent charity. In contrast, these organizations were part of a movement to change the world by creating a more sustainable form of capitalism. For them, success would mean that people could attain opportunities through work and good salaries, while also feeling connected to communities through volunteering and other engagement efforts at their own workplace. Corporate grantmaking and sustainability would funnel a portion of the money employees generate through their hard work to charities and causes connected to the areas in which their businesses operated. On an emotional level, I connected these goals with a sense of my own life trajectory. What if my mother had better health insurance? What if it had been easier for her to save and help me to finance my education without loans? What if more people just had the space to breathe and dream? That, to me, seemed as valuable as a million grants from the well-meaning private foundations of rich, old, white people. The traditional model certainly has a role to play, but this other movement might create a world that allowed more people to shape their own destinies and finance their own futures. The more I learned, the more it seemed to me that the whole world was going through a similar process to the one I'd experienced in my own life—a fundamental reimagining of how we could live and "do good" by making the world a better place than we found it.

I grew excited about this new vision for impact as I researched client programs and prepared briefings for client meetings. I called and corresponded with nonprofits in developing countries to obtain information useful in determining whether they were "legitimate" social-good organizations. If they were not (for example, if there were staff at the organization on the terror-watch list maintained by the US Office of Foreign Asset Control), their partnership with a major company could damage its brand and mission.

The work was fine, but more than anything I wanted to be noticed, to be given a chance, to be compensated. I continued to send in job applications. I created a strategic list of organizations, for-profit and nonprofit, that I wanted to work for, and then a list of organizations that they partnered with. My thinking was that if I could just get in with one of the organizations that my ideal employer partnered with, then they would be familiar with and supportive of the work that I was doing. This could open up options and lower a bar for entry that, despite my experience, education, and qualifications, seemed so impossibly high that I could not even get a single interview.

Things began to turn around. After almost three hundred resumes sent, I got an interview with J. C. Penney to be a CSR analyst. I made it to round three before I was informed that I hadn't made the cut. I didn't have any experience working outside the nonprofit sector, and my experience with analytics was mostly confined to economics work and research I'd done in grad school. I got other callbacks, yet none worked out. Still, I took these as a positive sign. I had committed to this gamble. These were steps forward.

Then it happened, *again*. Days turned to weeks, weeks to months. The wait. That familiar feeling of a future deferred. I realize now that it's not the wait itself that's the challenge. It's my impatience. I tried to shift my focus away from how fast I was moving in a given direction and toward measuring success by how close or far I was from the actual life I wanted to live, to measure velocity instead of speed, so to speak. I also reminded myself, as much as I could, that it only took one opportunity. Just one offer, and I could turn things around. That's a lesson I still take to heart.

I knew I wanted to live in a vibrant urban area. Let's just say the Bay Area, particularly the South Bay, didn't fill that need for me. Given rental prices that would make a Londoner blush and a lack of the kind of social scene that I enjoyed, I couldn't imagine how I would be able to build a life here. Yes, it was beautiful—the temperate weather, the fog rolling in off the sides of mountains. Yet it was still the case that with each passing day I had less and less enthusiasm for the long commute and the same-same weather. The leaves … didn't change. Forget about ever seeing snow.

Where would I go? Messay was thriving in grad school. We talked every day, but our conversations had become strained. I felt I wasn't doing anything, so I often didn't have anything to tell her about my work. And I wasn't about to tell her that my funds were running low or that I was eating bean and cheese burritos for dinner with the occasional Totino's pizza or a stop at Jack in the Box thrown in as a "healthy" treat.

Our lives were no longer really connected, and slowly we grew apart.

I took a job delivering pizzas to make extra money and felt frustration at spending more and more time on things that just helped me to get by. But I smiled and gritted my teeth. I had a bigger vision for myself. This was just a step along the way. I spent my time at the "returnship" learning. Wanting now to measure my velocity—my speed and direction—I started creating a formal map of this new ecosystem of "social good" that I was discovering. My map consisted of a set of locales that were familiar to me—big NGOs, governmental and multilateral institutions like the United Nations or USAID and the State Department. Having gotten clearer about the "why" behind my own motivations—my mission statement, so to speak—I also began to include a web of other organizations that were new to me but which I now understood were working to support these same goals. These were not only foundations and philanthropic organizations but also companies with social missions, some of them now calling themselves "B-Corps." There were also technology companies that innovated either to directly make a difference or to facilitate the good that other organizations and individuals sought to do. As an avowed nerd, this last category interested me beyond measure. In all my travels, I'd encountered so many organizations working so inefficiently. Technological innovation had changed the world around us dramatically, offering tools that made it easier to shop, to find good music, even to travel from point A to point B. What if tech innovation could also make it easier to do some good in the world? That simple goal had been so hard for me to find ways to achieve. What if it didn't have to be?

There in the office, working for free from sunrise to sunset, I learned more and more. I was not the first to have these thoughts, but they were a welcome distraction from my worries.

Just months before, the drive here had renewed my enthusiasm, perhaps even my will to live a life on my own terms. Yet as the months passed, I still felt that I had nothing to show for all my time and effort.

I knew this was the last gamble I had in me. I could feel the impact of malnourishment and stress on my body. That little gray patch of hair I'd started cultivating at the age of sixteen had grown exponentially larger. I couldn't *think* as clearly as I remembered being able to. It felt as if my mind, body, and spirit were exhaustible resources, and I was quite simply running out.

CHAPTER TWENTY-THREE

THE STRUGGLE

I arrived at the point where this story began: Rock bottom. Unable to cobble together the seven dollars I needed to take the train back home from the city.

I was stuck wandering the streets of San Francisco, my fate in the hands of JPMorgan Chase. I had spoken to the bank early that morning, and now there was nothing left to do but to wait. I walked for a few hours through city streets that had once invigorated me. I hoped to draw some life, some hope, from the sights and sounds of the city.

This time was different.

It wasn't like London, or Bangkok, or any other places and times when I was on a mission. In those places, my actions, my predicaments, and my responses all had a sense of purpose. All of them were hooked to a belief that if I could find my way through a particularly harrowing moment, everything would work out, and I'd land in a better place. In each of those moments, I'd been sure that my hard work would lead me to acquire the skills, experience, and resilience I needed to succeed. At least that's what I had always told myself.

But here, in San Francisco, whatever waning sense of mission I had left had detached from any sense of purpose. In its place, my self-doubt was thriving. After working hard for no pay then applying to job after job and striving to be recognized and given a chance and a voice, the hope that there was something better awaiting me was harder to cling to than it had ever been before.

As the hours passed that evening, I realized a sickening truth. There was no grand story to be told. I wasn't showcasing my resilience or building skills or experience. I was just sad, alone, hungry, ashamed. This wasn't an exploration of some new world or a new adventure. I wasn't invigorating myself or replenishing my energies from the vibrance of a dynamic and diverse city. I was just stalling for time, checking my account balance obsessively, hoping a few dollars spent in error on a Netflix subscription would magically reappear in my account. I was simply tired and scoping out spots to rest for the night on the concrete should the money not reappear on time.

This time was different because my hopes were all but dead.

As I walked the streets, I was acutely aware of all the homes I couldn't buy or rent, the restaurants with meals I couldn't afford to eat. In the midst of all that, my mind did what it does: I assessed my situation. It was warm at least. I wouldn't need to try to fight to be near a grate or to find a way to cover myself while sleeping. I wandered into the Tenderloin, a part of town near San Francisco's City Hall.

Like a lot of things in that city, the Tenderloin is a neighborhood with a reputation in the public imagination that stands at complete odds with what I know of its modern-day reality. I couldn't easily discern any charming art spaces, bright homes, or funky craft beer or cocktail scenes. It's hard to see those things when your eyes are focused on the street.

What I saw instead was entire blocks taken up by tents. It was as if entire neighborhoods had been turned out of their homes and pushed into just a few square blocks. The kind of urban lifestyle I'd so long craved seemed far from this place. The Boy Scout in me wandered those streets, looking for some safe and warm nook or cranny to call home for the night. As I searched, I mused: What I wouldn't give for my own tent in the woodlands of East Texas, far away from all this desperation and closer to that feeling of endless space and possibility summoned by my drive through the Texas countryside.

> WHAT I SAW INSTEAD WAS ENTIRE BLOCKS TAKEN UP BY TENTS. IT WAS AS IF ENTIRE NEIGHBORHOODS HAD BEEN TURNED OUT OF THEIR HOMES AND PUSHED INTO JUST A FEW SQUARE BLOCKS.

I found a spot along a wall in an alley that seemed cleaner than some of the others I'd passed. I sat and settled in with the dusk.

I think back often to this moment. I wonder why I didn't ask for help. Some of it was pride. I can't deny that. I'd worked so hard and received so much kindness already, including a whole life given for mine. How could I bring myself to ask for even more? Some of it was also a practical effect of life in a distressed economy. *Who* could I ask? My brother Will, with his own struggles to pay rent, pay for gas, find a new job, and support his mother? Messay, a graduate student with no job? My extended family? I'd never been particularly close to them, but I was close enough to know that they were likely struggling themselves to get by.

I had chosen my path. Made my choices. Taken my gambles. This was their consequence. I had failed to save the person that I loved most; all this was nothing less than what I deserved.

I was prepared to spend the night there. As dusk turned to dark and my phone was losing its charge, I checked my account one more time.

The funds had appeared.

Big finance had come through. I had just enough money to commute home on the train, and likely a couple of dollars left over for a burrito.

A few days later I stood on a Caltrain platform in Sunnyvale. I had gotten the latest pension payment from my mother. I was on the clock again, commuting back into the city. Unlike the previous week, I had enough to cover the cost of a two-way trip. The air was crisp. I remember, because as hard as things got, I could not help but cherish the crisp air of early fall and the sound of brittle leaves in a passing breeze.

I stood in bright sunlight staring off into the distance. I felt empty and foolish as a battle raged inside me.

It was time. I needed to stop what I was doing. The money was almost gone. I was down to my last pennies. I had lost weight and grown grayer. One-dollar 7-Eleven burritos were not meant as a primary means of sustenance. I had to give up. I had to take any job I could get that would allow me to pay my bills, to get off Will's futon, to just live.

But how could I? What would it all have been for? The risks I took, the stress I felt just working to stay on mission in Southeast Asia. Those months living in poverty in London, unable to find a place to live or afford a ride on the bus or tube; walking for miles just to go to class. Did my mother die for nothing? I would look on Facebook, hoping to be comforted by the smiles and adventures of friends, but their lives seemed perfect. Here I was with nothing, growing distant from the woman I loved, freeloading off the family I'd made for myself, applying everything I'd learned about how to analyze a situation and a problem to searching for safe and warm spots to sleep on city streets. I was a loser. A loser with a mother who had died ... for nothing.

Rock bottom: a literal description of the hard concrete I almost called home. Rock bottom: an unliftable heaviness in the heart and head such that one can barely muster the strength to move forward.

A commuter train was coming. I could hear it in the distance.

I was about six feet from the platform's edge. I inched forward. One inch. A foot. I was breathless and distraught. Too tired to shed another tear.

Another foot.

I was moving slowly as I had once before, when time slowed to a crawl during the foreign service officer exam. Staring straight ahead. My intentions and momentum intersecting with the approaching train. I couldn't live a life without purpose. If everything I'd done could have been for nothing, then what if I just ended this story here?

One more inch.

Thoughts of everyone I'd met. Everyone who'd believed in me and supported me. Their voices and their faces filled me up.

"If you do this, what would you say to her?"

I couldn't do it.

The doors opened. I boarded and broke down.

CHAPTER TWENTY-FOUR

A LiTTLe More OF SoMeTHiNg

Later that very same day, I received a call. One interview turned to two, then three. Once again, I waited. But for the first time in what seemed a long time, the count was in my favor. I had the job. It paid under $40K, and I would have to find the funds to move to Washington, DC, within a week. But I had the job.

I believe that relief, in its starkest form, is the emotion most akin to a tsunami. It washed over me with a force that few things have before. It was late September 2013. Just maybe, my story wasn't over yet.

I left my car in Will's care with a plan to make some money and pay to have it shipped. I was unsure whether it could make the drive. With some help from a friend who believed in me, I got a cheap Spirit Airlines ticket into Dulles. Her generosity was a timely reminder to me never to take for granted the people who can help and never to underestimate the willingness of those who say that they care and who offer to invest in a future for you. While it can often seem that our support systems are falling apart, we do still have each other.

The wheels groaned as we landed; I think everyone on board was shocked that they hadn't simply blown off. I boarded a shuttle bus to get into the city. The drive took almost an hour.

My third arrival in DC was nothing like the other two.

There was no quartet. There were no protesters. The Washington Monument and Capitol still towered in the distance. But the city was still and oddly silent. The city, and the country, was in the midst of something that would become more and more familiar to all of us over the next few years—a government shutdown.

Still, it was warm and sunny. Leaves were changing colors. I had come back to a land of seasons! All around, bars and restaurants were advertising shutdown specials. Their aim was to keep temporarily furloughed federal workers coming out on the town. I took it as a sign of good fortune. This might be a great time to be poor in DC.

I made my way to a hostel in Foggy Bottom (God willing, the last hostel I will ever set foot in as a guest). Thanks to my friend's generosity, I had enough money after buying the plane ticket to last me the couple of weeks before I would get paid. After months of pizza deliveries and working for no pay, the very thought of getting a regular paycheck seemed foreign.

I walked. The city was lovely. DC is a small place, with almost seven hundred thousand people crammed into about sixty-one square miles of land. In the daytime, as workers pour into the city, the population swells to well over a million people who stick around for happy hours and events. That transformation and its density makes it one of the most dynamic and interesting cities in the world to me. The metro was exactly as I remembered—a series of deep underground temples with high-vaulted ceilings dedicated to the worship of getting somewhere without having to rely on a car and pay for gas. The metro opened the entire city to me. I could walk and ride for hours and hours. I walked past monuments to ideals of grace and dignity. All around were people who gave off the same vibe as me. People on a mission, people with a purpose, people with endless ambition but not just for money or, despite popular perception, power. There were thousands working for small government agencies, for NGOs and foundations, think tanks and universities—all of them with a passion for the people they served. I thought back to that hunger for big ideas that had overcome me in my time as a radio producer and that had been satisfied in my graduate program in London.

This place was full of big ideas—some of them truly ridiculous, and some of them truly magnificent.

As I worked and was able to see more of DC, I also came to know a city that drinks way too much. Later I would come to learn that, in fact, its citizens drink more per capita than any other major US city. After all that I'd been through, and with all I still hoped to achieve, I felt I could use a drink. So I loved DC all the more.

Messay was also closer. I would ride the bus up to Pittsburgh to see her at Carnegie Mellon. After months of lukewarm phone calls and icy messages, it was a balm to see her beauty again in person and to see her thriving. She didn't know what I'd gone through, the dark thoughts that had crossed my mind, how close I'd felt to ending my story. Maybe one day, but for now, we had each other again.

Work, too, was a welcome relief.

I had discovered the company TRUiST (now FrontStream) during my time at the returnship mapping out the unexplored regions of what I would come to call the social-good sector. TRUiST built software that Fortune 500 companies used to manage their corporate social responsibility, including much of their grantmaking, and to engage employees around the world in volunteering and giving. The role I'd taken was an operations coordinator. Essentially, I built on the work that I'd done during the internship, vetting organizations for inclusion in engagement programs and for their eligibility for grants and partnerships.

Within a few months, I'd impressed my colleagues and been put in charge of the small team that handled charitable vetting in the United States and around the world. Finally, I'd been given a chance. I was going to make the most of it. In North America, there is a very clear database of eligible charities maintained by the US and Canadian governments. To add to this resource, I cataloged the countries in which we did the most vetting outside North America. I started with countries that had similar databases—like the UK, Australia, and South Africa. I also used my knowledge of international studies to expand the company's understanding of international regulations and treaties affecting the operation of nonprofits. Over time, I created a proprietary model that the company still uses to vet charities on everything from their responsiveness to potential ties to corruption. In my first year with the company, we trialed this new standard, and my new team vetted over forty thousand organizations. As a result, millions of dollars were distributed to organizations verified to be doing good work to improve communities. And of course, all this work opened up new avenues for partnerships between companies and nonprofits around the world.

There were also things I did through gritted teeth. At one point I had to lay off about two dozen contract workers who had for years earned some essential extra income at a crucial time of year (around the holidays), helping us contact and verify charities not listed in the IRS database and updating their records in our system. Leadership wanted to cut costs, so the contract workers' duties would be outsourced to India at a much lower hourly rate. With each conversation informing them of the news, I couldn't help but place myself in their shoes. The hard part of the recession wasn't over. Only now it was me causing pain to others. I wonder now how I did it. But I remember, too, how little choice I had in the matter.

I spent the next three months training a team of smart people based in India who nevertheless had a fundamental lack of knowledge about how charities operated in the United States/the West. They asked all the wrong questions, often gathered or approved the wrong documentation (for example, thinking common charities with different registered numbers from state registrations were entirely separate entities). It took a long time for them to become even 75 percent as efficient as their predecessors. Seeing this, I once again lamented a real economy that just didn't seem to be working according to the principles of efficiency—the principles I'd first encountered in shiny economics textbooks.

And then there was the data—both qualitative and quantitative— that lived in our systems. It was going completely unused.

Out of sheer curiosity and without asking for permission, I started to dig in.

I discovered a story of a girl suffering from a terminal illness. Her father had given thousands to the hospital in Ireland that was treating her. His company, US based, had a matching program to incentivize employee giving to charities. Yet they hadn't matched his donation because the charity wasn't approved. I did everything I could to vet the organization, allowing the company to match. I then shared with them the story, which had moved me to tears. They decided to make an even larger grant to the hospital in support of the girl's father—all because of a few sentences that had lived unseen in a spreadsheet.

This was surely not the only story we were collecting and not using. What if we built technology that helped bring this powerful anecdotal data more easily to people who had the resources and authority to change things for the better? That technology, and technologies like it, could seed the creation of a better world, where the good we can do is as ubiquitous as the products we can buy.

I thought back to being rejected from the corporate responsibility analyst role at J. C. Penney while I'd been in the Bay Area. I'd been told I didn't have enough experience in the for-profit sector or enough experience with data analytics. With this in the back of my mind, I took advantage of the moment, and I began to prepare reports. No one asked for them, but I did it anyway. I created reports on client giving, on trends in their grantmaking and volunteering. I investigated the kinds of causes our clients were supporting. I sought out notable comments and appeals for help that could be found hidden in the system. We'd seen the one-off example, but could we strategically push those stories to companies, matched to their own priorities, to spur even more good?

Looking back on it now, I was taking on a new mission. For some time, it had felt that my own voice, my pleas for an opportunity, weren't heard. Now, I saw that I had the opportunity to help some other voices rise above the fray. To help resources move more effectively to the people who really needed them. I realize now that this was always my purpose.

There was more to the picture than just my personal beliefs. Big data as we now know it was nascent. There were data that I was able to access then that might not be as available now, and for good reason. Yet a whole new world was opening up, not just for me but for everyone. I continued to map that expanded set of organizations. I set out to learn as much as I could.

Corporate social responsibility was a relatively new movement—even newer as a strategic concern—that sought to ensure that companies adopted practices that benefited people, planet, and profits. I created my own comparable value system—one in which I always try to act in a way that benefits community, career, and company (whether my own, a client, or an employer). These values changed the way I viewed work.

In learning all this, I saw a path to what might potentially be a more sustainable form of capitalism—one where my mother wouldn't have had to suffer such poor and uncoordinated healthcare, and one that wouldn't force people like me to take internships in expensive cities they could barely afford just to have a chance at a dream. Could there be a form of capitalism in which fewer and fewer people would find themselves standing at the edge of an abyss and pondering an end to their stories? Could we waste far less human potential by ensuring that people had jobs and nutritious food to eat?

As the months went by, I settled into a housing arrangement with five other young people on Capitol Hill, just blocks away from the Supreme Court and the Capitol. I lived in a literal closet and would stay there my first two years in the city. My head touched one wall and my feet the other. Everything I had in the world fit in a small dresser beneath my bed. I had one small window out onto the world. Eventually the cherry blossoms bloomed. It was a stunning sight, like walking among and underneath clouds.

After a time, the work I'd dived into began to be recognized. I was promoted to head of Research and Analytics, a brand-new team built on the foundation of the work I'd started. I cleared other milestones to find purchase for my ideas, including speaking at the company's annual conference and in other venues about my research and the impact of the company's growing suite of products.

I even managed to get my car shipped from the Bay Area to DC. Will packed it with everything else I'd left behind and loaded it onto a truck. It took every penny I'd saved since arriving in the city. After a four-day trip clear across the country, there it was, dirty but still beautiful. That car had taken me through plains, deserts, and mountains on a journey to my opportunity.

It was also what kept me feeling close to my mother. Though I'd bought it with my meager inheritance for a whole mix of confused reasons, shame not least among them, it was also one last gift from her. Along with the small hundred-dollar pension I still got every month, that car symbolized to me that my mother still had my back.

In September 2015, I got my first credit card so that I could get a new suit and new tires and drive up to Pittsburgh for Messay's graduation from Carnegie Mellon. Driving on the Pennsylvania turnpike, top down, I smiled. I had a job connected to purpose. I had new friends and a place in a city I loved. I had my beautiful, little, used Pontiac Solstice. I had a beautiful and brilliant partner.

Messay's graduation from Carnegie Mellon

Life stabilized. The occasional payday loan and pressures of a life lived paycheck to paycheck had by no means become strangers to me. But as my mind cleared, the feeling I had was akin to awakening. I realized that my every waking moment, whether conscious or not, had been full of anxiety, self-doubt, and fear that I'd once again find myself adrift, with no work and nothing but a dream I'd never achieve. I'd been burdened for so long by overwhelming doubt, questioning every decision I made and every principle I'd chosen to adhere to.

In my life experiences, I'd learned multiple meanings of freedom. There was freedom that came from financial stability and opportunity. There was the kind of freedom that came from hearing and being heard, from having one's existence, ideas, and overall value acknowledged. Then there was the freedom that came from open spaces, from disconnecting from crowded spaces and day-to-day activities. Finally, there was freedom from anxiety and worry—whether about oneself or others. I'd had precious few moments of any, let alone any hope of feeling all four simultaneously or of discovering even more.

A few months after she graduated, Messay moved to the city, and we got our own place, even though I had grown to love my housemates. This was especially true of my roommate Molly, who I admired for being a champion in her policy work for social security and those suffering, like her grandmother, from Alzheimer's. She had quickly become one of my greatest friends. It was hard to leave. But moving out was the beginning of a new chapter.

With more space to breathe, I came to understand more of who I wanted to be and the broadening options and choices available to me to become that person. The jobs and titles I'd obsessed over straight out of school seemed smaller parts of a much bigger world. I knew now with certainty that I wanted to do impactful work to increase other people's chances of living well—to more quickly and efficiently get them the resources they needed to have a chance at success. I knew that I also wanted to be creative and to innovate. And I knew that I wanted to be an active part of a broader dialogue involving big, exciting ideas for improving the world.

> I KNEW THAT I WANTED TO BE AN ACTIVE PART OF A BROADER DIALOGUE INVOLVING BIG, EXCITING IDEAS FOR IMPROVING THE WORLD.

There's nothing like being newly focused. Filled with enthusiasm and renewed hopes, I charted a course deeper into the new territories I had discovered. I expanded my map by creating a running list of notes I labeled "Future" that contained all the organizations making the world better in ways I felt I could believe in. That had come to include a much wider array of organizations than I would have thought when I first started down this path; now social impact of any kind—new products, socially sustainable investments, or traditional philanthropy—might be found on my map. I also tracked titles and roles I might have at these organizations as well as the places these organizations were represented—conferences, events, webinars, even happy hours.

Then there were people—connections I could make to further broaden my understanding and learn of new opportunities. I read up on the studies and research that potential connections produced or referenced in their work. I recorded it all in my "Future" notes. I devoured everything I could find, reached out to anyone who would respond, monitored every organization on my list for new openings, and attended and applied to speak at any event I could. What started as a simple map transformed into an entire methodology that I now pass on to mentees or others struggling to find a path.

CAREER MAP

1. **INITIAL QUESTIONS:** Begin by digging deep into questions like why you have the ambitions you have, why you do what you do, why you love and hate the work-related tasks you love and hate, what would be an ideal role, and what you would want people to say about what you've accomplished and why.

WHAT DO YOU LOVE? WHY?

_____
_____
_____
_____

WHAT DO YOU ENJOY DOING? WHY?

_____
_____
_____
_____

WHAT DO YOU HATE DOING? WHY?

_____
_____
_____
_____

IDEAL ROLE?

_____
_____
_____
_____

YOU'RE DYING—WHAT DID YOU ACCOMPLISH? WHY?

_____
_____
_____
_____

2. **MISSION STATEMENT:** Examine your own answers to these questions to find key words, phrases, and concepts that reoccur and resonate with you. Use them to complete a draft of your mission statement.

I do _____ to support (cause/population/organizations) to/that (outcome) and (action) to / that (your why).

3. **TITLES/KEYWORDS:** Examine what types of roles and job titles do the kind of work described in your mission statement.

_____
_____
_____
_____

4. **COMPANIES/ORGANIZATIONS/INSTITUTIONS:** What kinds of companies have these kinds of roles and do work that's connected to your "why"?

_____
_____
_____
_____

5. **PEOPLE:** What kinds of people are in these organizations or are now or have been in these roles doing work that resonates for you as connected through your mission statement and your "why"? These are people you should try to meet.

_____
_____
_____
_____

6. **CONFERENCES/EVENTS:** Where are these roles, organizations, and people? In what events, venues, etc. do they meet?

_____
_____
_____
_____

7. RESEARCH: What research is relevant to your mission statement? What do these institutions publish? What publications, articles, etc. do these people read?

_____
_____
_____
_____

8. RECRUITING/COACHING: What training and coaching is common for people in these roles? For people with the same "why"? What, if anything, is offered by these organizations?

_____
_____
_____
_____

NEXT STEPS & TIPS

Once you've done this, iterate on and try to internalize your mission statement for use in your interviews and conversations.

You might find people at companies or conferences the companies sponsored or attended, and then add companies that they interact closely with/present with/partner with.

As you come across research, people, institutions, add them.

Use this as a map to help you think of where to go, whom to visit.

I was relentless in doing everything I could to connect with the points on my map and create new opportunities for myself. It's true that I was still racing, still impatient and afraid of falling behind. I remembered how I'd felt run over by life before, and I dreaded a repeat of those times when whatever fire was in me had almost gone out. But now that I could feel the fire's warmth again, I also had a clearer sense of direction that helped me to combat those anxieties. Some part of me knew that it was all just a *new* gamble but now, after so long, I also felt I had … something? Yes. I had something. Just a little more of something each day.

CHAPTER TWENTY-FIVE

THE SEEDS OF MY FOUNDATION

I stayed at the company just under two years before leaving to another of the organizations on my growing map of the social-good economy. I would be the research manager at the Council on Foundations. Operating as *the* national association for philanthropy, the Council conducted research into best philanthropic practices, provided legal advice, and advocated for the thousands of public, operating, corporate, and private foundations that work in communities across the country and around the world.

I'll never forget the day I received the offer. I was expecting the call, so I took the day off. I tried to occupy myself with Netflix, washing dishes, sweeping the floors over and over. When the call finally came, around midday, I jammed my phone to my ear as the head of HR laid out the terms. Fearing a loss of reception, I moved as close to our window as I could, as if the offer and the joy that came with it might evaporate.

They say you should negotiate. And there's truth to that advice. Yet there's also truth in the overpowering feeling of true gratitude and perspective. Perhaps I'm alone in this thought. Or perhaps others who've suffered through their own kinds of loss and scarcity will understand. I was too grateful to negotiate. Too fearful that this chance would just disappear. Instead, I stood with my hand over my mouth. Silent. They'd offered me almost double my current salary. This was the moment in which I might truly break free of abject poverty. Perhaps it might yet be possible to achieve one of those kinds of freedom.

I hung up the phone. I jumped and jumped and jumped. And for what felt like the millionth time on this wild journey to something better, I wept.

The job was a revelation. I was able to interact with, provide research to, and take an active part in conversations with almost every organization on my growing map. The Council's members ranged from local community foundations to large entities like the Gates Foundation as well as the philanthropic arms of companies like Johnson & Johnson, Blackbaud, and IBM.

My map also grew. In my time at the Council, I led one of the largest studies ever done into how philanthropy is amplifying its social mission through "impact investing." You see, foundations typically do their good primarily through their grantmaking, but that giving generally constitutes only 5 percent of their total assets. The other 95 percent or so is invested through their endowment. It sits in accounts, growing so that the foundation can continue to exist and pay staff year after year. Impact investing—new to me and just becoming a growing practice—involved organizations using their endowments to invest in companies and funds that did no harm (think divestment from fossil fuels) or actively sought to do good through proactive environmental, social, and governance (ESG) practices. Think of all the good philanthropy achieves through grantmaking. Now imagine as much as 80 percent of those endowments, 1,600 percent more dollars, unleashed to improve the state of the world. The work was exciting.

I also led the organization's research into diversity, equity, and inclusion in philanthropy. And as I dug into the world's largest and most continuous trove of data on the gender and race of staff within corporate, public, and private foundations—data going back over thirty years—I understood more clearly than ever why I had struggled to gain access to roles within the sector. The data were clear.

I didn't fit the profile.

Whether through implicit bias or outright discrimination, women, mostly white women, filled the ranks of the program officer roles, and white men occupied the leadership positions. According to the data, things had been this way for decades. Worse yet, at the rate of change seen over ten years of detailed data on staff demographics, it would take decades for women to become as common in leadership roles as they were among the ranks of program officers. Any sense of change was an illusion.

I was struck by the thought of a whole sector of our economy, one charged with investing in a better future, devoid of change. Innovation was changing everything about our world. Yet in every way these organizations were old, sclerotic, slow, and fearful of anything *different*. They were unwelcoming. Even in instances where they wanted to change, instances I encountered through interactions with these institutions on phone calls, in meetings, or at various convenings, I began to question how they could even begin to innovate without a full range of perspectives and ideas. More broadly, what did it even mean to engage in social good if only a few voices defined and got to engage in that work? Whose world would we end up building and reinforcing?

Just as my map had broadened my mind beyond the limited roles I'd imagined for myself early in my journey, this research broadened

WHaT DiD iT even mean To engage in social good iF only a Few voices DeFineD anD goT To engage in THaT work? WHose worLD WouLD we enD up BuiLDing anD reinForcing?

my perspective even further. The job of defining a better world should not belong to any one person or category of people. Yet that was what we commonly called philanthropy and social good. To me this meant two things. First, there was a limited understanding of what philanthropy truly meant. So many people hunger to improve their neighborhoods and communities. So many long to create a better world than what they see all around them every day. So many work hard to help others avoid the hardships they've overcome. The resources they offer are substantial, perhaps even invaluable. Many had helped me on my journey. Yet we apply the label of "philanthropist" to the limited few with the privilege to contribute in very prescribed ways. To my mind what followed from this was the second thing: the simple idea that just as there are people being left out of philanthropy, there were organizations and industries being left out as well. I had to expand my map even further.

I spoke at more and more conferences, received more and more invitations to publish articles and join panels. I realized that traditional philanthropy was not the place for me. In many ways, the typical foundation represented everything I opposed: organizations underpinned by money they wouldn't have in a world with more equal opportunities; institutions striving to reshape our world into something imagined by a few privileged elites and the limited voices around them, a cacophony of homogenous perspectives.

As much as I'd learned over the years, as much as I'd worked to expand my understanding, I was still the same at my core as when I first felt driven to toil away with nothing but a hope and a prayer that my work mattered. Please don't misunderstand. Traditional philanthropy is essential. It can and does make a difference and drive positive change. Yet it cannot be the way that we create the worlds I want to help create.

In other words, Jean-Luc Picard would not be impressed.

After a year at the Council, I received an invitation to join a sixty-year-old NGO based in Alexandria. They were starting a technology company called Growfund, an innovative giving platform. They wanted me to join as a senior director of their social-good consulting group and to lead the new platform, which had received an investment that included over $600K from the Gates Foundation.

In my new role, I consulted on social-good projects with some of the largest companies, foundations, and nonprofits in the United States and around the world. I even led a project reexamining the efficacy of the Combined Federal Campaign, the largest employee giving campaign in the world, which sends millions to charity. I also built a new product focused on creating a platform to "democratize philanthropy." The product was the brainchild of Scott Jackson, the organization's CEO at the time. At Growfund, we wanted to expand access to donor-advised funds (DAFs), charitable giving accounts that allowed individuals to contribute assets, gain a tax deduction, and then from their fund make grants to charities. Essentially, DAFs enabled individuals and organizations to create their own private foundations. These funds had exploded in popularity. By 2017, one fund provider, Fidelity Charitable, overcame the United Way Worldwide to become the largest charity in the world.

Instead of spending millions to establish a foundation, DAFs could be set up for around $10,000. Of course, even at that lower price point, they were reserved for the wealthy. Through innovations spurred on by Scott—as well as Ann Canela, the VP who led the consulting group and, after seeing me speak in various venues, had recruited me to lead the Growfund initiative—we managed to reduce the cost of establishing a DAF to just $1. With Growfund, we thought—I hoped—we had an opportunity to expand the idea of what it meant to be a philanthropist. Having just left the atmosphere of privilege and exclusion at the Council on Foundations, I couldn't have been more excited for the work.

I envisioned young poor kids like me saving just a few dollars a month for their own foundations and funds. I saw them growing older and using the funds they'd set aside to support nonprofits in their community. I pictured poor parents using the same tools as the wealthy to create funds that they could manage with their children, learning and discovering, as I had, organizations that inspired them to be and do more. I envisioned groups of ordinary people banding together to fund the organizations that big philanthropy overlooked. I hypothesized that with the right incentives and structures, our technology could function like savings accounts, encouraging ordinary people who might not otherwise give *at all* to save just a little at a time and make grants to fund their own philanthropic goals. And just like savings accounts lead to new financial opportunities and knowledge, these funds would become the seeds for learning about giving strategies, exploring charities in local communities, learning about volunteer opportunities, or finding jobs within socially sustainable companies.

Most of all, as usual, I thought of my mother—the small pension I received each month, how she had sacrificed so much to allow me to explore my own vision of the world. I set up a fund in her name: the Gwendolyn Smith Charitable Fund. The pension goes there now. Her gift to me is my small gift to the world, the seeds of *my* foundation.

I spoke at dozens of conferences over two years. I managed and grew the entire team and our technology product. I was a committed evangelist for our vision. While we succeeded in growing the fund and even launched a giving circle-focused iteration of the platform that continues to grow steadily, I grew frustrated.

Donor-advised funds have come under intense scrutiny. It's said that they "capture" funds that would otherwise go directly to charities. More and more, as I worked and traveled the country to engage on the topic, I came to see this limited view as a reflection of the elitism that surrounded the traditional philanthropic space. In their function, DAFs were no different than the 501(c)(3) charitable organizations established by Bill Gates and other wealthy donors. No one argued that *those* institutions "captured" funds that would otherwise have gone to charity. Instead, often rightly, the funds that seeded traditional private philanthropy were viewed as the bedrock of an individual, family, community, or corporation's sustained commitment to their own vision of a better world over years and decades.

What accounted for the difference in perception? Were the super wealthy more capable of sustained commitment than ordinary donors? Charities bent over backward to steward and cultivate relationships with large foundations and high-net-worth donors. Could they not do more to create high quality relationships with ordinary people in their communities? There were barriers but also new technologies and new ideas. Why couldn't this become a goal? I felt increasingly alone in believing that every day people had a right to the same tools as the wealthy, the same role in shaping the long-term future of their communities.

I became so engrossed in all this that over time I lost Messay. I was so focused on my mission and on trying to make her proud, something I now know is an unhealthy habit of the way I understand love, that we grew apart. Ironically, she got a job as a program officer within a large DC foundation. She was helping to provide grant funding to institutions like the Kennedy Center and some of the largest arts institutions in the world, as well as to some of the smallest organizations serving the people of DC. I was certainly proud of her, but we had built wholly separate lives.

Messay had been there for me when my mother passed, for days and nights of conversations during my time in London. For so long, a life with her had been something I longed for. Yet I was so focused on getting to a place where I could sustain my new mission financially, that I'd begun to take her for granted.

At other moments in my life, I would have spiraled after losing her. I would have believed that I was totally and completely alone. This time, I had begun to acknowledge that there was love and support all around me. I took solace in new friends, new adventures, and I placed all my focus on not losing the fragile freedom I'd finally achieved. That freedom was everything to me—even with one less person to share it with.

I got my own apartment overlooking one of those iconic DC traffic circles, right in the heart of the city and just a few blocks from the White House. I loved to hear the traffic go by. That rush I'd felt in Bangkok, in London, all around the world—it was part of my every day now. The life I'd wanted was real. It worked for me. Now it was all that I had.

It was 2015 when I got rid of my last pair of shoes with holes in them. I wonder if anyone ever noticed the water that seeped in on rainy days as I'd strolled around San Francisco and DC. The leaks. I like to think of that small event as the end of my beginning. It was most certainly not the end of my story.

CHAPTER TWENTY-SIX

THe Same, BUT DiFFerenT

My hands were shaking. Just a bit. Sitting backstage in the dark, I placed them on the table in front of me and took a few deep breaths. There had been so many rehearsals—day after day, on the phone and in person, for weeks. Now it was time. I could hear all the familiar lines just on the other side of the massive black curtain. I hardly needed to, but I checked my watch. Still fifteen minutes before we were up.

I traced the path of two of the speakers as they walked by. Were there cords in the way? Equipment? How embarrassing would it be to fall? Another speaker walked by. And then another. As our turn approached, I felt a familiar sensation. It was the same feeling that I had before every presentation, speech, or panel, and every gig. No matter how large or small the audience, every step up onto a stage is preceded for me by a kind of out-of-body experience. A sense of surprise that it's me and not someone else taking those first few steps, not tripping and embarrassing himself in front of CEOs, VPs, and CTOs at the world's largest companies, stepping past the curtain and standing on stage. Then suddenly it's me again. I'm the one standing in front of a crowd of thousands. I'm the one looking out at representatives of nonprofits and companies from around the world, all gathered in a packed ballroom at the Hilton in San Francisco's Union Square, all there to see what I and my team had built.

It's 2019, and the setting is Dreamforce, the world's largest technology conference. It's easy to get lost among the almost two hundred thousand attendees. Saying it's overwhelming to be part of such an event doesn't begin to cut it.

I'm standing on stage at a social impact keynote leading our product demo; beside me is a colleague and a client that she's interviewing. My role is small, nothing to write home about. But I'm here, looking out past bright lights, listening for the cues we've agreed on. I helped to envision and build the product. I was a lead in the effort to craft a compelling story around it that would help this audience and any of the millions who were viewing the live stream to understand what we were trying to achieve. All in all, this was not too different from my days in a band, coordinating with my bandmates to get the music just right. This product had just as much of my love and passion invested in it as any song. Hopefully the similarities ended there. I could live without anyone asking if Tracy Chapman built it.

We announce a slew of new innovations we believe—I genuinely believe—have the potential to begin a movement of innovations that fundamentally change how people connect to charity.

The presentation is a success. Without having said a word, I smile and wave to the audience, retreating back behind the curtain.

There are smiles and celebrations. The sun sets, and I find myself taking familiar steps through the dusk-lit streets of San Francisco's Tenderloin.

I visited San Francisco almost once a month during this period. To be truthful, each time it was worse than I remembered. The entire city was a neon sign advertising the perils of income inequality. It was a message writ large on every street corner, every block taken over by tents and the blank stares of the hopeless.

I would meet those eyes as I walked by. My heart would sink as I responded "No, I don't have any cash" to those who asked. I envied them for having the courage to ask. I still sometimes wonder how my path might have been different. There were so many times I just didn't—couldn't—bring myself to ask for help. And yet I had been the recipient of so much help.

I felt proud that my gambles seemed to have paid off and that I had become a respected participant in a mission shared by many. Yet in that place with its slowly dimming light, I was also aware of my doubts, of my lingering internal conflict. I felt transported to the past. I found myself walking by that same alley where I'd once planned to spend the night. I can't say this was the first time I'd come by here; it probably won't be the last. I stood and revisited that moment from the past, before there was a ramen shop on the spot. I saw myself there. Crouched down. Head on my knees. My own hopeless eyes scanning my phone, waiting.

I breathed deeply, and I walked back to the hotel. So much has changed.

I was recruited from Growfund to be a director of product, building social impact solutions within Salesforce, specifically Salesforce.org, the company's social impact division. I was one of the first product minds to be brought on board to shape the vision for what was at the time Salesforce's newest offering, Philanthropy Cloud. It's a product that leverages the same AI and machine learning tools that help us more easily find music and movies to help ordinary people, within companies and eventually in any setting in the world, find a way to more easily engage with social good—as a volunteer, a donor, an advocate.

In many ways Philanthropy Cloud is a version of the vision I had with Growfund, a tool to facilitate funding and supporting the future that ordinary people, not just the wealthy and the super wealthy, want to bring into existence. The product was also aligned with what had solidly become my own mission, to unleash and through technology streamline the movement of tremendous resources—money, time, attention, and more—to the people and causes that need them. I envisioned and built all the volunteering-related functionality on the platform. Occasionally, I daydreamed that the technologies and principles we implemented and the ways they change society by making the act of charity a part of everyday life might one day be a listing in the archives of a future USS *Enterprise*.

Then in mid-2020, as the COVID-19 virus raged, I was put in charge of wellness and well-being solutions on Salesforce's new Work.com platform. My team built solutions to help companies get back to work safely and healthily. I also developed and got buy-in for a vision for wellness and well-being within the workplace that supports workers more fully than ever before. The product I outlined and got greenlit would work similarly to Philanthropy Cloud by leveraging data and AI to understand what employees need to feel happy, safe, and well at all times at work. It would gather that data through surveys and other tools, then match them to the resources they need—whether nonprofit services, employee assistance programs, mental health or fitness-related benefits—as easily as they get matched to causes on Philanthropy Cloud, movies on Netflix, or products on Amazon. Better work. A better world.

In December 2020, I received an offer to become a leader within Facebook's social impact team. The opportunity would allow me to focus on vision and strategy for a team that has built new fundraising tools, like the ability to "donate birthdays," inviting friends to donate to a favored cause in place of giving a gift. They had built this kind of functionality to take advantage of the scale of social media and distribute billions to causes around the world. I grew excited at the thought of achieving similar scale for volunteering, for advocacy, for impact investing, and everything people might want to engage with to help make our world a better place. There was little question in my mind about the unrealized potential of these new platforms to help do good in the world, at a minimum by making social-good interactions like giving and volunteering a part of the kinds of everyday social interactions that so many participate in on Facebook, Instagram, WhatsApp, and beyond.

At the same time, I received a counter-offer from Salesforce to return to Philanthropy Cloud and start and lead the corporate social responsibility "Industry Solutions" team. In this role I would help conceptualize how various Salesforce technologies, working as a whole, might serve as solutions for every way a company would want to do good in the world for its stakeholders. How might they innovate? What partnerships—with philanthropic research institutions and others—could drive corporate impact? This work would include being part of conversations on innovations to a growing suite of products helping companies help the world, including Philanthropy Cloud, Sustainability Cloud, Work.com Wellness, and more.

I agonized over the decision. In each case I could have very distinct impacts through my work—on companies and their countless employees, suppliers, shareholders, and nonprofit partners, or on the everyday social-good decisions of billions of daily users of Facebook. I lay awake at night, unable to sleep.

In the end, it became clear that the Salesforce opportunity was not only a great chance to innovate and move more resources to people who need them—to be a part of having impact at incredible scale—but also it would provide continuity that would allow me to take care of and be there for Messay when she needed me.

I might still be someone who's driven to seek what's next. But the form of that journey, I realized then, had changed for me. I felt free from the trauma of scarcity that drove me to neglect so much of what I loved. And so it was that, in the moment I settled on the Salesforce opportunity, it truly struck me just how much had changed, how far I had come from that darkness. How many more choices I had in the recession of 2020 than in the great recession.

And those choices do abound. I'm an entrepreneur. Messay and I became business partners on a startup called goARTful. Conceived as a "Rent the Runway" for art, the idea has evolved into a vision for putting art from local artists inside local businesses. We put meaningful local art on the walls that benefits local causes through a charitable fund we established and manage through Growfund. It's a product and a dream that, like so many small businesses and startups, faces an uncertain future in a rapidly shifting world where even offices may become a thing of the past.

I'm also an investor and a consultant for equity, having started to work as an angel investor under a brand and project I call Democratize

Ventures.[6] My goal is to invest in entrepreneurs of color and products that democratize access to art, philanthropy, donor-advised funds, or social networks and community for people who otherwise would be shut out of those worlds. To help others who've struggled as I have, I use the product and research expertise I've built up to advise startups and small companies for equity and occasionally pro bono, and I provide career advice for those looking to ask "why" and dig deeply into their motivations, the career they want, the map of the space they want to work in, and the impact they want to have on the world.

This work has led me to a myriad of investments, including owning a small stake in a bar here in DC. There's no piano for my mom to play, but the bar is built out of old metro cars, and the space will promote local art and artists and encourage conversations on equity and urban renewal. I also have a stake in a few other startups—a fashion company called Voor that will digitize the fashion supply chain and make it easier for diverse creatives to build fashion brands, and an app (tentatively called the Regular) that will allow people to more easily join new communities by "subscribing to the places they love to go and the things they love to do at the push of a button."

So much has changed. So much remains the same.

The coronavirus pandemic may seem novel, but what's quite familiar is seeing our leaders turn essential short-term tactics like social distancing into long-term strategies. As I write this, those we should look to for guidance have no plans, offer no inspiration or innovation, and certainly show no welcome for all the different kinds of expertise that could help us think three steps ahead. So

---

6   Democratize Ventures provides pre-seed funding of $10K-$20K annually to entrepreneurs with products that match our interest areas. We also provide career advice for those looking to transition to entrepreneurship, as well as product advisory services—occasionally pro bono or for equity—at www.democratizeventures.com.

many have lost their jobs and are struggling to arrange shelter, to find a meal. Offering up basic truths should be a given; instead, it's become a heroic act.

But so many have curtailed their activities to protect our communities—one of the most profound acts of charity I've ever witnessed.

so many Have curTaiLeD THeir acTiviTies To proTecT our communiTies— one OF THe most proFounD acTs OF cHariTy i've ever wiTnesseD.

So much remains the same in me as well. I still descend into my own wells of fear, where the darkest thoughts pool and grow stagnant and poisonous. I continue to have the thought that everything I've worked for and built could come crashing down in a heartbeat. I have specific recurring nightmares about homelessness and hunger. I still struggle with the thought that I'm not good enough or the uncomfortable awareness that I spend so much time focused on my mission that I can sometimes fail to take care of the ones I love, the ones who make my world a place worth living in. My worries and fears are an ever-present shadow that both tempers and sweetens life's pleasures.

Still, I have found more personal peace. And I still strive. Even in 2020.

Early in the year—just before the coronavirus hit—I put in a contract on a penthouse condo. That had always been a dream of my mother's, granted one that was always beyond our reach. And while I've never been one to believe in the rather limited vision of the American dream that revolves around home ownership, the idea of her dreams dovetailing with mine made the moment my offer was accepted powerful for me.

I found myself experiencing a kind of déjà vu as the pandemic forced me to wait to close on and move into my new home. In many ways, it called up that very familiar feeling of a dream deferred. Now, however, I know that waiting is part of my journey and that my own growing patience and perspective have great influence over how much pain that waiting causes me. It's a lesson I wish we could all learn.

Messay and I have gone through so many dizzying ups and downs over the decade we've been in each other's lives. In summer 2020, we traveled with a small group of friends to a small farmhouse in the Shenandoah Valley for a brief weekend of respite from Washington, DC, a place, like many, ravaged by the pandemic, by peaceful but boisterous protests, and by hateful politics that had mobilized soldiers and troop carriers out into the streets. Taking a moonlit walk on the farmland, Messay and I gazed up at bright stars, much brighter than in the city, and a bright crescent moon. The silhouettes of nearby mountains and hills loomed over what we could still see of the horizon. The world was quiet, save the crackling of a nearby fire and the laughter of a few close friends.

I proposed to her on that warm summer night. She said yes. The world we get married in will be a much different world from the one in which we met.

I also find myself, like you might be as you read this, witnessing and experiencing another global economic crisis calling up issues that extend far beyond my own little world. People are dying. Essential workers are making impossible decisions in service of others. Millions of people are losing their jobs every week and, with those jobs, the healthcare that sustains them. I've looked out at empty streets in the once-vibrant city I now proudly call home, only to see the few people out and about afraid to be close to one another. It has seemed, at moments, that civilization is coming to an end.

I hope that in my story there may be some kernel of truth that helps you if you are struggling through hard times. I hope that my story enables you to see your way through to another moment or helps you just to take another deep breath. I hope reading this book might help you think through how you can hold on to a dream that could change lives or change our world for the better. I hope it helps you to come to your own understanding of freedom rather than to accept whatever you've been told will set you free. I hope this book might help you clarify the life that you wish for and confirm your right and your will to strive for yourself, for those you love, for your community. Most of all, for anyone who might find themselves in the coming months and years at their own rock bottom, on the cusp of decisions driven by the unique despair and hopelessness that accompanies the feeling of complete and utter economic ruin, wondering about your place in a world where all your dreams and hopes seem indefinitely deferred, to you I say this: Times are hard. But don't give up.

Maybe you can't afford a proper meal. But don't give up.

Maybe you have to take risks you never imagined you'd have to take. Don't give up.

Maybe everything you've worked for seems to be crumbling. Don't give up.

Maybe you've lost someone or something dear to you. Don't give up.

Maybe your dream demands to be rethought. Please don't give up.

Keep hold of your bright future. Be willing and able to ask yourself hard questions like "Why do I want the things I want?" Remember to open up your definition of success, of impact, even of "good" rather than accept what's imposed on you by those who won't even listen, or really hear, your story. The future you want—and the world we create together—probably won't look much like Star Trek or any fictional future universe. It might be better. It might be worse. Either way, it can be a world we create together.

Right now, I'd say that world may be our collective dream deferred. It's a dream I don't mind waiting for. It's certainly a world for which I'll join you in the fight.

CHAPTER TWENTY-SEVEN

FiNDiNG YOUR WAY TO THE OTHER SIDE

When volunteering as a mentor, I draw on all of my experience to try to help provide my mentees with some clear tools for finding their way through a crisis and getting closer to a life they want to live. Make no mistake: If you're struggling as you read this but holding on to the embers of a dream that may well be deferred through no fault of your own, you are facing the core of the crisis.

It's likely you will find yourself choosing between actions that help you live your life today and actions that may not help you today but will set you up for a better life in the future. Look no farther than the culture of unpaid or low-paid internships for evidence of how, too often, these two priorities find themselves at odds. Personally, I've come to believe that carefully navigating my way through that conflict was at the heart of my most daunting struggles and any freedoms I've found for myself.

I want to return to something I wrote earlier about the limits of human productivity. As a human being, you have those fifty productive hours in a given week. Ask yourself: what can you do with that time?

Yes, you need a job as an adult (and sadly, often in this world, even before). You need to pay your bills, put food on your table, have a place to rest. Yet that's just the beginning of your journey. You also have a dream.

I think it's so important to imagine all the ways—*any way at all*—to connect that dream to the tasks you're engaged in to meet those basic needs. What does this look like in practice?

Imagine you're working as a bartender but have a dream to be a jewelry maker. Maybe you get agreement from the owner of your bar to bring together some other jewelry designers for a once-a-month showcase that includes your own work. When you keep in mind the limits of human productivity and how valuable your time is, every single hour you might spend as a bartender in that bar that is also time spent in an environment making connections to others who can provide advice, experience, feedback on your creations, or any connections to the kind of life you still dream of living—any of that is an additional 2 percent more time you're able to bring the power of *focus* to your efforts to build that different life. These things all become data points for you to complete your own map of the space you want to inhabit and be successful in. It's a map that is driven by your mission and includes the organizations, titles, people, events/conferences/gatherings, and research/knowledge that live within it. All these can help you to grow in ways you may not even expect.

I believe that anyone who goes down this path can find ways to balance their needs with their desires so that more and more of the life choices they need to make to survive will intersect with the dreams and passions they desire to truly thrive. Then maybe, if we're lucky, those of us who follow this path will find ourselves someday spending 100 percent of our time on things we love as part of a life we *chose*.

There are also tools I believe have been invaluable to me. As it turns out, many of these tools for escaping the darkness are tools and philosophies that are also used to build successful products.

The first tool is exploration and opening yourself to new and big ideas. Open yourself to the "why" of everything and the many different ways a goal can be reached. In my exploration of big ideas, the most important thing I have learned is to forget about what's been deemed possible or feasible. You can build and begin to populate your map *and* engage in the act of exploration. When building products, product managers and entrepreneurs participate in meta-studies/research of articles as well as interviews with stakeholders or thought leaders with a deep well of knowledge and expertise about the field or industry into which the product will launch. During this exploratory phase, we don't ask what "realistic" problems potential customers and users might want a product to help solve for them. Instead, we ask what interviewees and other customers and users in a given space would want from an *ideal* product. When using this tool, we cast aside any thoughts limited by what's realistic and focus instead on *what's desired*. Then we build a plan to get to that ideal point in phases with the resources we have available. Life is no different.

My exploration was greatly facilitated by my travels around the world. I saw and experienced places I couldn't have dreamed, careers I'd never thought to imagine for myself. That said, you don't need to take a trip around the world to reap those benefits. You can arrange quick twenty-minute phone calls with people with different jobs (think April Ludgate in season seven of *Parks and Recreation*, which I hope for your sake you have watched). You can watch documentaries. You can go to lectures. You can read various job descriptions. However you do it, explore and keep opening your mind to all the possibilities that are before you. Cast aside what you think is possible for you and simply ask: What is my *ideal*?

Second, forget job titles and the traditional frames that are in many ways forced on us. Job titles are meaningless when it comes to exploring the life you want. Instead, pay more attention to job functions. In my case, before and after graduate school, I was obsessed with job titles and a career with an international NGO, the State Department, or the United Nations. I wanted titles like Deputy Chief of Party and Country Analyst. That meant anything less was bound to feel like failure. But then I took a step back. I tried to break these roles down to working descriptions of the job functions. I came back again to the "why": Why do these roles exist? What are they designed to achieve? And what about that action or function did I find appealing? This is similar to the product-building phase in which ideas and descriptions are written to describe the general function of a given feature—to answer the questions: what does the feature do, and why is it important to someone?

> However you do it, explore and keep opening your mind to all the possibilities that are before you. Cast aside what you think is possible for you and simply ask: What is my ideal?

In my own case, it became clear that the "why" of all the roles I was interested in had to do with coordinating the efficient movement of resources for social good and the development of people. At heart, I wanted to help create those better worlds I saw in the science fiction that had moved me as a child. I felt that reaching toward a better world would require a greater proportion of humanity getting the resources necessary for reaching their full potential. When I eventually stepped back even further, it became clear that other job titles in other industries involved many of the skills I had and had the same impact—they fulfilled that same purpose of more efficiently moving resources to where they needed to be. The recognition of similar job functions allowed me to be much more flexible about my path and to create a career focused on coordinating the efficient movement of resources through various technologies and innovations like social enterprises, impact investing, and building social impact-focused technology products. This has involved a shift from my original conception of how I might make a difference to a whole new world of opportunities in technology, corporate social responsibility, philanthropy, and community-building. It's also helped me to see what I think so many miss—a career has nothing to do with a job. A career is who you want to be, eventually who you can say you are. It's independent of company, role, or anything of the sort. It's the collective output over time of all the things you end up doing, tied together with a narrative thread. In other words, it's something that is endlessly customizable and flexible in a postindustrial world driven by information and continuous learning.

Third, and finally, it's vital to build a meaningful network. There are inequalities in network access that must be seriously addressed at a structural level, but networking is also easier than ever with LinkedIn and other social apps and tools. Once you have explored and have a better sense of your ideal and the meaning or impact you want to find through your work, find others who have gotten to where you might want to be. Read their bios. Learn from the path that they took to get to that point. In keeping with the distinction between "job" and "career," more often than not you'll find that their paths are not nearly as linear and clear-cut as we're taught to imagine or as many people—retroactively—make it seem. This aspect of building a life is similar to competitor research in product management or entrepreneurism. Just as someone in those roles would not seek to replicate existing products, you do not need to replicate the paths that others have built for themselves to achieve the life you want. The inspiration you draw from others' lives should never overshadow the fact that you are your own person.

You have your own journey and your own story.

A New Mission

My journey has been one of continuously formulating and reformulating the principles by which I live. I'm constantly asking myself "why" I want what I want and "why" I think what I think as a means of getting to the core of what lies underneath my ambitions, my self-doubts, my fears, and my joys.

I started off with a set of principles and a dream for the impact I wanted my life to have. Things didn't go as planned, but I now have that impact—I help build tools for a better world, tools that help unleash human potential by more easily moving resources to people and organizations who need them no matter where they are in the world. As I emerge into all the freedoms that I sought, I have nurtured new goals:

- I want Democratize Ventures to evolve from a project that funds $10K–$20K per year of my own funds to a full-fledged venture fund for social enterprise startups that support entrepreneurs of color and democratize tools once reserved for only a few or for the wealthy.

- I want my mentorship as a volunteer and through Democratize Ventures to help young people see what's possible for them through careers that do more than make them money. I've spoken publicly about that new kind of capitalism. And while I believe tools like what I built and visioned for Wellness through Salesforce Work.com have the potential to pave the way, it's ordinary people and employees looking for companies and products that are positively tied to social concerns that will bring about that revolution.

- I want to champion *against* unpaid internships that make it too hard for many who are interested in building a career and sustaining a life improving the state of the world. I also want to be a champion for more diversity, equity, and inclusion in organizations that receive taxpayer support to carry out their missions. We now know through copious data that products with diverse perspectives are better built; so, too, are futures.

- I want to use technological innovation and creative thinking to capitalize on this nascent drive for a new kind of capitalism and to solve social problems. Recognizing that income inequality powerfully affects our chances, I want to tackle issues like affordable access to higher education and affordable housing using some of the same tools that big companies use to solve problems and be responsive to the sometimes huge populations of users and customers they serve. These tools include design thinking, product management techniques, innovative feedback channels, and agile methodologies.

- I want to participate in the creation of a compassionate healthcare system. When employment is tied to health outcomes, losing a job can mean losing access to the resources that can save your life or the life of someone you love. If anything has made clear the need to divorce the healthcare system from the free market, it's the coronavirus and the crises that its unabated spread has caused throughout 2020.

I've wanted a life that was a good story. I've wanted that from the time I walked nervously through that huge gate and past that perfectly manicured lawn into my first job out of college, to the times I struggled to survive in Southeast Asia, to the times I struggled in London and San Francisco just to find my place and voice. I still want that story. As my life moves into a new phase, I know clearly that what will make my story a good one is if it helps others to have a good life.

The world may be big enough to crush us, but we can be for one another the gravity and balancing forces that keep us from falling or floating off into the darkness.

ACKNOWLEDGMENTS

I was recently told a story by a mentor, Bill Patterson (executive vice president and GM leading Salesforce CRM), of how he'd been asked once in an interview how he would move Mount Fuji. His answer was, "Stone by stone." I'd like to acknowledge people who helped me grow and move toward a brighter future stone by stone:

Kimberly Haley-Coleman, founder of Globe Aware—you helped the world open up to me.

Sylvia Komatsu of KERA and Krys Boyd of the NPR program *Think*, airing nationally out of KERA—from you I learned the value and the art of a good question, patience, and the power of ideas.

Ann Canela, Scott Jackson, Austen Brower, and the incredible team that had my back with Growfund—from you I learned how to advocate for a product and build a team to support it.

Nick Bailey, Jon Stahl, Dave Manelski, and Margo Mayes, the amazing minds behind Salesforce's Philanthropy Cloud—I learned with you the freedom and power that comes with being able to truly think *big* about impact.

ABOUT THE AUTHOR

Brandolon Barnett is an innovator, author, and entrepreneur. He helps build and lead products, initiatives, and partnerships that bring together tech and social impact to move resources to people who need them. He is currently head of Corporate Social Responsibility Industry Solutions in Salesforce.org's Philanthropy Cloud and leader of the Democratize Ventures investing and advisory initiative. He has succeeded and failed as startup founder, promoted development and volunteerism on three continents, led the Gates-funded Growfund donor-advised fund effort, and participated in research and consulting engagements at the Council on Foundations and Global Impact. He has spoken at SXSW and numerous other venues. He loves karaoke and the Dallas Mavericks and lives in DC with his love Messay Derebe and cat Logan.

DEMOCRATIZE
VENTURES

I'm sharing my story in the hopes that it helps someone to see the light at the end of the tunnel in dark times. It's not the only way I hope to help. I founded and lead as a volunteer a project called Democratize Ventures (DemocratizeVentures.com). Based in Washington, DC, Democratize Ventures has two main goals:

- To support products, programs, innovations, and investments that unlock the movement of resources to the people who need them

- To support the democratization of products, programs, innovations, and investments so that they are available to new groups who struggle to find equal access as entrepreneurs, employees, program starters, and innovators

Democratize Ventures offers this support in three ways:

- Pre-seed-stage angel investments of between $10K and $20K to organizations fitting the above investment criteria

- Product advisory services offered pro bono, for equity, or for a fee

- Career and brand design for entrepreneurs of color offered pro bono or for a fee

Democratize Ventures won't support products, programs, innovations, and investments that don't have a vision and strategy at every phase to make social impact (in one of its many potential forms) core to their mission, but I'm happy to help *anyone* think through how to get there. Visit DemocratizeVentures.com to learn more.

LinkedIn: Linkedin.com/in/brandolon

Twitter: @BrandolonB

Instagram: @bbrand0

Facebook: Facebook.com/BrandolonB

Printed in the USA
CPSIA information can be obtained
at www.ICGtesting.com
JSHW012023140824
68134JS00033B/2849